Lost Attractions
═ OF THE ═
SMOKY MOUNTAINS

Lost Attractions
OF THE
SMOKY MOUNTAINS

TIM HOLLIS

Published by The History Press
Charleston, SC
www.historypress.com

Copyright © 2020 by Tim Hollis
All rights reserved

Front cover, top left: Becky Craddock collection; *top center*: Mitzi Soward collection; *top right*: author's collection; *bottom*: author's collection.
Back cover: author's collection; *top inset*: author's collection; *bottom inset*: author's collection.

First published 2020

Manufactured in the United States

ISBN 9781467144124

Library of Congress Control Number: 2019956044

Notice: The information in this book is true and complete to the best of our knowledge. It is offered without guarantee on the part of the author or The History Press. The author and The History Press disclaim all liability in connection with the use of this book.

All rights reserved. No part of this book may be reproduced or transmitted in any form whatsoever without prior written permission from the publisher except in the case of brief quotations embodied in critical articles and reviews.

Contents

Acknowledgements — 9
Introduction — 11

One: Hillbillies and Indians and Bears, Oh My — 13
Two: Misplaced Mirth and Mayhem — 41
Three: Kings of the Wild Frontier — 79
Four: This Way, Please — 107
Five: Putt It There, Pal — 125
Six: A Dramatic Conclusion — 147

Bibliography — 171
About the Author — 173

In the pages that follow, we will be seeing dozens of Great Smoky Mountains attractions that no longer exist. But the view captured in this incredible mid-1970s aerial of Pigeon Forge is also a sight that no longer exists. Note the comparatively barren roadside landscape of U.S. 441, looking south toward Gatlinburg and the mountains. Tiny motels abound, with only the concrete volcano of the Magic World theme park (*lower center*) hinting at the explosion of attractions yet to come. *Author's collection.*

Acknowledgements

Although most of the material you will see in the pages that follow originated in my own decades-long collection of memorabilia, credit must be given to the additional sources that enlivened the result. As you will notice in the credit lines for the photos, a number of them come from fellow tourism collectors and photographers: Shelia Atchley, Billy Baker, John Burgess, Becky Craddock, Bob Howard, Butch Hudson, Loren Jones, Joy Stout Jucker, Jeremy Kennedy, Brian McKnight, Mark Pedro, Warren Reed, Katie Sidwell, Mitzi Soward, Skylar Spake, Jerry Thompson and Cyndy Woller. We must also acknowledge the late photographer John Margolies, who bequeathed his personal archive to the Library of Congress with the amazing stipulation that no restrictions were to be imposed on its use by other authors and researchers.

The author's first visit to the Smokies was at age three in August 1966. In the left-hand photo, you can see him and his family when the world was still in glorious black and white, having lunch at Gatlinburg's Howard Johnson's restaurant. The right-hand photo was taken in 1985, at which time Simple Simon and the Pieman were still hanging at HoJo's as if nineteen years had not passed. *Both, author's collection.*

Introduction

Welcome, friends, to the latest volume in the ongoing Lost Attractions series. For those who are new in this neighborhood, perhaps it would be best to begin by explaining the title. Just what is a "lost attraction" of the Great Smoky Mountains, anyway? Well, it is very simple. A lost attraction can be any type of tourism-related business—roadside attraction, motel, restaurant or other—that no longer exists. Casually flipping through the pages, one may conceivably run across an image and comment, "Hey, that place is still there!" That would bring us to the secondary definition: a business that has changed radically over the years and no longer resembles its depiction in vintage photos and postcards, even though technically it may still be operating. Everything clear now?

My own personal connection to the Smokies goes back to when I was three years old. Apparently, by that time my parents had decided that I was old enough to withstand the environment of a road trip, and for reasons that are now unknown to me, they chose the Smokies as our initial destination. Judging from the photos my dad shot with his trusty 35mm camera on the trip, it appears that we saw Gatlinburg only by passing through it, spending most of our time on the other side of the mountains in Cherokee. Maybe the fact that my mom always loved Western movies had something to do with it, but considering how badly she hated any kind of vacation trip that meant leaving home and her beloved cats, I doubt that Cherokee's appropriation of the customs and costumes of the Plains Indians had any influence on our itinerary.

INTRODUCTION

Looking back through the lens of history, what is really bizarre is to realize that at the time of our visit (August 1966), Smokies tourism was only about thirty-five years old. The geographical isolation of the mountain country had ensured that hardy farmers had been scraping out a living in the valleys of the Smokies for centuries with very little contact with the larger outside world. For the well-to-do people in Knoxville, the nearest city of any size, the communities of Sevier County—including Gatlinburg, Pigeon Forge and Sevierville—seemed to be quaint reminders of a bygone day. It was this thinking that prompted the Pi Beta Phi sorority to establish a school in Gatlinburg in 1912, first, to help educate the uneducated, and second, to establish an arts and crafts program to preserve the way the mountaineers had been doing things all along.

Crafts—of the mountain variety on the Tennessee side and Native American on the North Carolina side—drew some tourists into the isolated region, but it was when the Great Smoky Mountains National Park was established in bits and pieces between 1934 and 1940 that the tourism industry really got started. Improved roads, allowing access to the new national park, had a lot to do with it, and by the time World War II and its travel restrictions were over, the region was ready for success. Now, let's pile into our Chevrolet and see what the USA once had to offer in those formerly sleepy Smoky Mountain communities.

CHAPTER ONE

Hillbillies and Indians and Bears, Oh My

We will begin our tour of the Smokies' lost, if not completely forgotten, attractions with the most logical ones: the places that made at least an attempt to tie themselves to the region's native culture. On the Tennessee side of the mountains, that translated into bears and hillbillies; crossing the national park via U.S. 441 brought tourists into an alternative universe where bears remained but their human counterparts were Native Americans—not always, however, the ones who had occupied that land for hundreds of years.

The attractions and other businesses that employed these stereotypes were among the first to spring up once the area had discovered that there was gold in them thar touristers. While handicrafts were the initial draw on both sides of the mountains, it did not take long for business owners to latch on to the depiction of mountaineers and American Indians as portrayed in motion pictures, animated cartoons and comic strips. Bears were yet another matter. As we shall see, they were often depicted in their natural state, but even more frequently they were caricatured into a cartoony form that would have been quite at home with Yogi and Smokey and their fellow ursine celebrities. Turn the page, and you will begin to see what we mean.

Makin' "a run" of corn likker at Homespun Valley

OPPOSITE: Gatlinburg's first attraction not connected with crafts was Homespun Valley Mountaineer Village, a reasonably accurate re-creation of life in the hill country before the encroachment of tourists and national parks. Homespun Valley stuck around until at least the early 1970s, but its former property on Airport Road now boasts Gatlinburg's civic center complex. *Author's collection.*

ABOVE: Farther north on U.S. 441, Hill-Billy Village arrived in the even sparser environment of Pigeon Forge around 1954. Primarily a souvenir shop, it grew to include many other exhibits. It was not loath to employ every conceivable hillbilly stereotype in its signage and other iconography. *Author's collection.*

ABOVE: By the time Hill-Billy Village opened, the traditional cartoon hillbilly had been well established by comic strips, including *Li'l Abner* and *Barney Google and Snuffy Smith*, as well as the magazine panel cartoons of Paul Webb's *Mountain Boys*. All of these figures appeared at Hill-Billy Village in the form of wooden cutouts adorning the displays. *Author's collection.*

OPPOSITE: As the signage on the "largest still ever captured in Tennessee" explained, what the public thought of as hillbilly culture was not exactly a thing of the past, with that particular example having been confiscated in 1962. Considering the public's interest in seeing long-dormant stills, it should probably be no surprise that the legal moonshine industry fuels many attractions in Sevier County today. *Both, author's collection.*

LOST ATTRACTIONS OF THE SMOKY MOUNTAINS

ABOVE: After more than six decades in business, Hill-Billy Village closed after its 2016 season, and in July 2017, the garish yellow building and all of its exhibits were bulldozed into oblivion. In November 2018, the former site looked like this, with the traditional sign still looming overhead as a memorial. *Author's collection.*

OPPOSITE, TOP: What was the Hillbilly Museum? Where was the Hillbilly Museum? We can tell you that it opened in May 1968, but now you know as much about it as the rest of us do. (Note that, as with many pre-1970s ads, this one has to tell people that Pigeon Forge is between Gatlinburg and Sevierville; otherwise, they might pass right through it without noticing the community.) *Author's collection.*

OPPOSITE, MIDDLE: The hillbilly image was not confined to attractions and souvenir stores; restaurants also cashed in on the reputation of old-timey mountain grannies for good home cookin'. This one in Pigeon Forge resembled the later mega-successful Cracker Barrel chain, but it retired to its old rocking chair many years ago. *Author's collection.*

OPPOSITE, BOTTOM: Far from the ballyhoo of the U.S. 441 strip, at Townsend, "Wilson's Hillbilly Restrunt" attempted to out-mountaineer all of its kinfolk. Its advertising consisted almost entirely of dialect, promoting its "fride chicken" and "ho-made bread." And maintaining its good humor, this postcard states that the establishment is owned by "John and Norma Wilson and our friendly banker." *Author's collection.*

HILLBILLY MUSEUM

Y'all Come And See...

THE MOST EDUCATIONAL ATTRACTION IN THE GREAT SMOKY MOUNTAINS

—FEATURING—

Thousands Of Primitive Articles Of Yester-Years. DON'T MISS IT!

PIGEON FORGE, TENNESSEE — BETWEEN GATLINBURG & SEVIERVILLE

OPPOSITE: Now, let's switch from hillbillies to bears, which were residents of the Smokies before any human beings found the region. Motels and restaurants could be counted on to use the shaggy black beasts in any possible form, from the realistic to the cartoonish. As you can see here, while tourists were strongly forbidden to feed the bears, there was no law that said bears could not feed the tourists. *Both, author's collection.*

ABOVE: People who came to the Smokies did so fully expecting to see bears in the wild, and if they could not always be glimpsed in the woods, at least they could be seen alive. The location of this particular roadside stop is unknown, but it appears that one of the ursine denizens of the area was doing his bit for the visitors. *Author's collection.*

There were several locations where live bears could be seen together in a zoo-like setting. Both of these were in Pigeon Forge. The Three Bears Gift Shop technically still exists, but this neon-bedecked pink and mint-green structure burned several years ago and was replaced by a more modern version that bearly (haw, haw) resembled the old one. *John Margolies collection; author's collection.*

ABOVE: Sometimes, bears continued to entertain even after they were no longer able to eat, or move around, or breathe. This rather bizarre example of taxidermy stood on the Astroturf sidewalk in Gatlinburg in the 1970s. *Butch Hudson collection.*

OPPOSITE, TOP: Following the winding route of U.S. 441 across the national park brought carloads of tourists to Cherokee, North Carolina, the center of an actual reservation. Around the same time that people discovered the native crafts of Gatlinburg, they also latched on to the Native American culture of Cherokee, and the reservation would never be the same. *Author's collection.*

OPPOSITE, BOTTOM: The strangest thing about Cherokee's version of tourist culture is that it largely ignored the tribe's genuine past in favor of a Plains Indians look that was based on the image seen in Western motion pictures (and, later, television shows). By the 1950s, Cherokee's main drag looked like it could have belonged in Albuquerque or Sioux City. *Author's collection.*

ABOVE: A Cherokee tradition that has not died off completely is the unique profession of "chiefing," or dressing in the elaborate garb of Plains Indians and posing for photos with tourists for a fee. The Cherokee "chiefs" can still be found, but their settings are quite different from the ones seen in these vintage views. (And just drool over that classic Kentucky Fried Chicken ad on the billboard.) *Author's collection; Brian McKnight collection.*

OPPOSITE: This unusual "double" postcard shows a couple of different angles of this Cherokee souvenir stand. At the top we can see its otherwise traditional assortment of wares, but at the bottom we see its parking lot full of photo-op statuary. Pay attention to that gaping green dinosaur, as we will be meeting him again later. *Author's collection.*

OPPOSITE, TOP: The Cherokee tribe did not live, sleep or eat in the traditional cone-shaped tepees of the Plains Indians. But as with the elaborate feathered outfits worn by the street-corner "chiefs," that fact did not prevent the image from turning up over and over again along the tourist strip. *John Margolies collection.*

OPPOSITE, BOTTOM: The Fort Tomahawk souvenir store is still very much in business but no longer features this stockade-style exterior. For a perhaps even more outdated view, check out that corner with its oversized yellow boxes of Kodak film. When was the last time you saw any of that stuff? In the century before this one, maybe? *Author's collection.*

ABOVE: Although this business has shut down, the giant chief seen here in 2005 is reportedly being preserved in storage and will someday be able to give his stereotypical "how" greeting at some other location, hopefully in the not-too-distant future. *Author's collection.*

OPPOSITE: When Cherokee's giant Harrah's Casino was built, it was a financial smash, but it forever changed the streetscape around it. The Chief Motel was one of its neighbors that fell to the wrecking ball. Across the street, the neon chief's daughter watched forlornly as her namesake Princess Motel faced its own doom. *John Margolies collection; author's collection.*

ABOVE: Down the road from Cherokee at Whittier, the Warrior Motel sign managed to look more threatening than welcoming, with the neon arm waving its tomahawk back and forth. At last report, the former motel was serving as an antiques shop. *Brian McKnight collection.*

OPPOSITE: Not only did the Cherokee-Rama unexpectedly turn up in Gatlinburg rather than in North Carolina, but it also might have been the only attraction in the Smokies to advertise by making fun of its own name. The artwork on this brochure hardly indicated what was to be found inside the building. *Author's collection.*

ABOVE: Indoors, the Cherokee-Rama presented a miniature landscape on which tiny figures acted out the tragic story of the removal of the Cherokee tribe from its native lands. The same owners were responsible for the very similar Confederama at the base of Lookout Mountain in Chattanooga. *Author's collection.*

OPPOSITE, TOP: Aunt Mahalia's has been cooking up goodies for Gatlinburg visitors since 1939 and continues to do so. But the sweet old auntie no longer does so in this gingerbread house–type building as seen on a card postmarked in 1956. *Cyndy Woller collection.*

OPPOSITE, BOTTOM: The Maggie Country Store in Maggie Valley is often cited as one of the inspirations for the ubiquitous Cracker Barrel restaurant chain (although at least one or two other roadside fixtures can also claim part of the lineage). Examining this photo carefully reveals some classic examples of 1950s and 1960s product packaging, which today is as antique as the era the country store represented. *Jeremy Kennedy collection.*

ABOVE: East of Cherokee, as U.S. 19 winds its way toward Maggie Valley, there are numerous examples of small motels that found themselves unable to survive in the changing tourism world. This aqua-colored sign at one of them is slowly being reclaimed by the mountain foliage. *Brian McKnight collection.*

ABOVE: It seems easy to guess the story behind this "retouched" view. Apparently, Hyams Gift Shop sold out to Roper's Jewelry and Gift Shop, which decided to keep using the existing stock of postcards by trying to black out the store's original name wherever it appeared. But Hyams was stronger than ink and has emerged from hiding, while the Roper's name is fading into the background. *Author's collection.*

OPPOSITE: Starting as a tiny gift shop, the Rebel Corner grew to be a major attraction in the heart of Gatlinburg. Its décor was certainly meant to show tourists that they were not in Boston or New York City. It is somewhat surprising that the store did not ask to be paid in Confederate money. *Warren Reed collection.*

OPPOSITE: One name that was seen on signage everywhere in the Smokies, but particularly in Pigeon Forge, was that of former college football player Charles "Z" Buda. He was credited with helping many entrepreneurs with the start-up of their own businesses, but Buda had his fingers in so many other pies that it is impossible to keep track of them all. His hilltop campground was one of the last to bear his name, long after his death in 2004. *Both, author's collection.*

ABOVE: Why would Lums Restaurant be considered a part of local culture? No particular reason, except that the hot-dog chain was originally named after a popular 1930s and 1940s radio comedy serial, *Lum and Abner.* Since the two title characters ran a general store in a rural setting, they could be considered a part of the same craze that produced Hill-Billy Village and Wilson's Hillbilly Restrunt, even though their humorous misadventures took place in Arkansas' Ouachita Mountains rather than the Smokies. *Author's collection.*

CHAPTER TWO
Misplaced Mirth and Mayhem

While the attractions we have just visited often exaggerated the true nature and appearance of native mountaineers and Native Americans, not to mention turning wild bears into furry, friendly greeters, all of them at least made an attempt to fit into the world of mountain culture. But there was another genre of tourism that quite deliberately went in the opposite direction, and it is to those myriad attractions to which we now turn a sometimes baleful eye.

Someone once said that the whole idea of the tourism industry was to make people feel like they were someplace else when they were already someplace else. In Florida, this often translated into a business going after a South Seas or Polynesian theme, even when geographically that culture had no connection with the state. Perhaps it was the same line of thinking that caused attraction owners to develop themes that were quite deliberately counter to the usual sights to be found in the mountains. How else could one explain the preponderance of tropical-themed porpoise shows, whimsical fairylands, haunted houses and other such misplaced merriment? These strange and often unexplainable sights take up more space than any of the others discussed in this book, so take a deep breath and prepare to plunge into a weird world unlike any you might have seen before.

What were the main things people came to the Smokies to see? Of course, there were the mountains, then, hillbillies, bears, Indians, porpoises, hula dancers—whoa, back up thar, sonny! Yes, Pigeon Forge's Porpoise Island looked like it belonged somewhere in Florida, and the public must have agreed. Its life was short, but while it lasted, it certainly provided employment for more performers of South Seas ancestry than anywhere else in the region. *Both, author's collection.*

ABOVE: Performing porpoises, trained seals and bikini-clad emcees did not enjoy a long stay in the Smokies, but Porpoise Island's reputation lives on. Its former site is still an entertainment complex known as The Island, but otherwise, the thrill rides and other attractions there have nothing to do with the tropics. *Shelia Atchley collection.*

OPPOSITE: Hard as it may be to believe, porpoise shows in the Great Smokies went back further than Porpoise Island. This one dates to the mid-1960s, and there was another one in Maggie Valley at around the same time. Apparently, the well-being of the marine mammals was of secondary importance. *Author's collection.*

Tennessee Porpoise Circus

PIGEON FORGE, TENN.

– CHICO –

– SMOKY –

– L B J –
(Lady Bird Jumper)

First Show 9 A.M.
On The Hour Thru 5 P.M.

NIGHT SPECTACULAR
At 8:30 P.M.

—FEATURING—

THE ASTRONUT'S

COMEDY DIVING TEAM
An Exciting Underwater Show

Special Admission Price

ABOVE: If Pigeon Forge could clone Florida's trained animal shows, it could make its own Cypress Gardens, right? Actually, it was Wisconsin Dells tourism mogul Tommy Bartlett who decided to bring his brand of water-ski spectaculars to the mountains in 1978, and it began with the construction of an enormous stadium overlooking an even more enormous artificial lake. *Author's collection.*

OPPOSITE: Water-skiers and bikini-clad beauties might have been dandy for Florida and/or Wisconsin, but in Pigeon Forge, their careers were as brief as their swimsuits. By the early 1980s, Tommy Bartlett's show had packed up its skis and retreated to the Wisconsin Dells, where it remains a tourism fixture today. *Both, author's collection.*

THE
Tommy
Bartlett Show
PIGEON FORGE, TENNESSEE

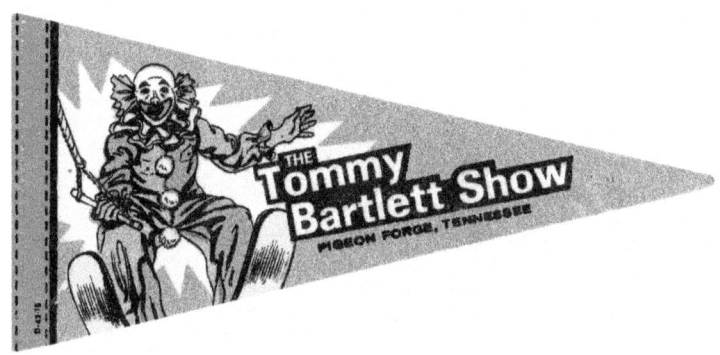

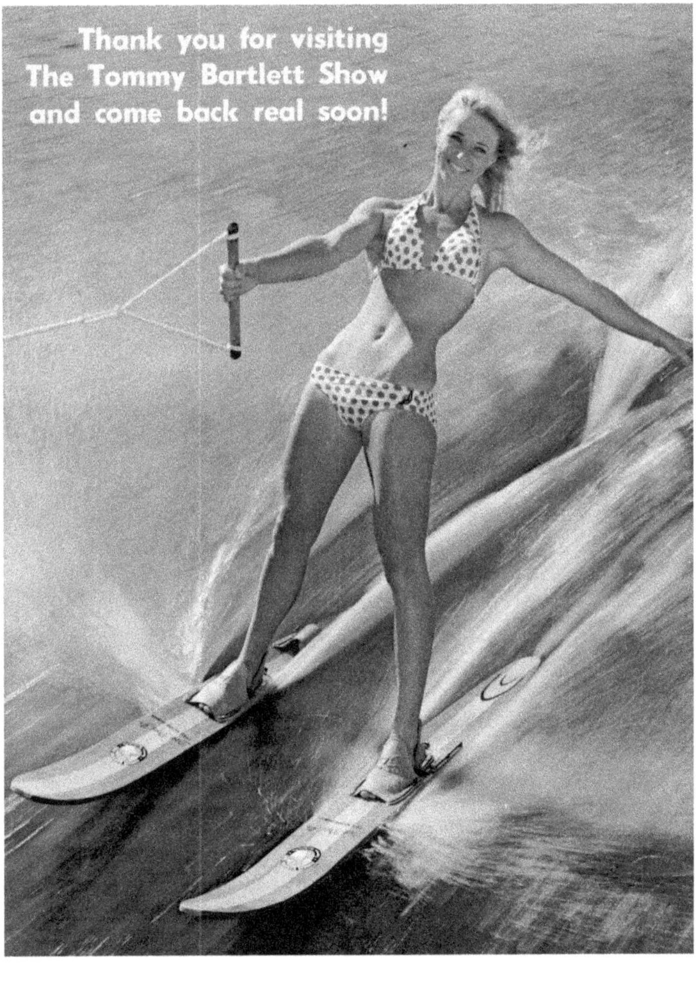
Thank you for visiting
The Tommy Bartlett Show
and come back real soon!

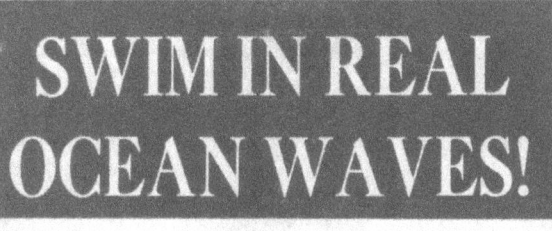

OPPOSITE: Today, the former Tommy Bartlett stadium and its bleachers can still be seen, with the former water-skiing lake a patch of manicured green grass. But just wait until chapter six, where we shall see what happened on that property during the years immediately after the departure of Bartlett and his performers. *Both, author's collection.*

LEFT: There was seemingly no end to the attempts to bring Florida to the Tennessee hills. As this brochure explains, the oxymoronic name Mountain Ocean was given to a wave pool that simulated the pounding surf of the beach. *Author's collection.*

ABOVE: Even without crashing waves, water parks proved a profitable way to give tourists a chance to cool off during the summer heat. Sevier County's pioneering Ogle family had one of the longest-running and most successful of these aquatic attractions. *Author's collection.*

OPPOSITE: Even Cherokee could not avoid the craze for water parks. These remnants of a teal-painted waterslide can be seen on a hillside above a snack bar, but locals' memories get fuzzy when asked when the park operated, or even its name. *Author's collection.*

ABOVE: Naturally, most motels offered their own swimming pools quite separate from the water parks. The Royal Townhouse in Gatlinburg parked its pool on the roof, along with the prerequisite Florida-style bathing beauties. Daisy Mae and Daisy Duke had some competition in those hills, it seems. *Brian McKnight collection.*

OPPOSITE: Gatlinburg's Mystery Hill was little different from all of its gravity-defying relations in other tourist areas; however, its non-secluded location—it was not even on a hill—might have rendered it a bit less mysterious than the rest. *Author's collection.*

LOCATED ON U.S. 441
Next to JOLLY GOLF
at the north edge of
GATLINBURG, TENNESSEE 6/1/7

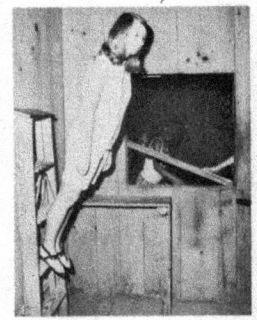

Visit the Mystery Hill and see many astonishing things that seem to defy the laws of nature. Here the law of gravity seems to have gone berserk and your sense of balance is entirely upset. Many theories have been offered such as, earthquakes, magnetized mineral deposits, fallen meteorites, deflections of gravitational force and many others. We invite you to visit Mystery Hill, experience these natural illusions, and offer your theories. It's entertaining for young and old. Tours are conducted by courteous guides and last about 15 minutes. Open April 1 through October 31.

OPPOSITE, TOP: All of the standard "gravity spot" illusions could be spotted at Mystery Hill, including the supposedly level floor that gave visitors a new slant on the whole business. *Bob Howard collection.*

OPPOSITE, BOTTOM: In the early 1970s, Mystery Hill had to have a new set of postcard photos taken to reflect changing styles and fashions. In contrast to the earlier "farmer's daughter" look, here we see two girls from the *Brady Bunch* era discovering their first growth spurts. *Author's collection.*

ABOVE: The idea of a "live ghost" show seems a bit ironic to begin with, doesn't it? Gatlinburg's long-running Hauntings theater was indeed the haunted home for creepy creatures, which appeared on cue throughout the stage show. *Author's collection.*

EXCITING—EDUCATIONAL
FORT WEARE
GAME PARK

Young and old alike appreciate and enjoy the fine entertainment of the animal acts.

*W*e sincerely hope that you will enjoy your visit to Fort Weare and this vacationland region of the fabulous Great Smokies, comprising our country's most visited National Park. Here you will discover there's plenty to see and do.

*I*t will be much appreciated if you will show this folder to a friend back home who might later be traveling this way also.

*W*e are always glad to have the chance to explain the various features of interest about Fort Weare, and to tell about the other sightseeing attractions of our area, or supply other visitor information.

On 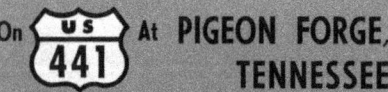 At **PIGEON FORGE, TENNESSEE**

EXCITING—EDUCATIONAL
FORT WEARE GAME PARK
IN THE SMOKIES VACATIONLAND

EXOTIC ANIMAL WONDERLAND
On **US 441** At **PIGEON FORGE, TENNESSEE**

NEAR THE SMOKIES RESORT TOWN OF
GATLINBURG

MAGGIE ZOO and REPTILE FARM
Featuring animals and reptiles from both the Americas.
Rattlesnakes milked for venom.
ENTER OF MAGGIE, N. C.   OPEN MAY THRU OCTOBER
Larry Mathis, Owner & Operator

OPPOSITE: Zoos and similar animal attractions flourished in the days before the welfare of their exhibits became more of a concern. Fort Weare Game Park was one of the earliest—and one of the largest—in the Smokies. It operated from at least the mid-1950s into the late 1960s, and its sizeable property later swapped its live animals for concrete beasts as the location of the Magic World theme park. *Both, author's collection.*

ABOVE: Over the mountains in Maggie Valley, this small attraction kept growing like an elderly alligator. Eventually morphing into the Soco Gardens Zoo, it became a mainstay of the area's tourism for many years before crawling back into the underbrush in 2006. *Author's collection.*

ABOVE: It seems that anywhere there was a mountain, someone had the urge to develop transportation to the top. The Cherokee Sky Lift was one such attraction, leaving the busy tourist strip below for a round trip straight up. *Author's collection.*

OPPOSITE: Some sky lifts, including the one in Gatlinburg, have continued in operation for years, but in Cherokee, this was all that remained of its ride in the spring of 2019. One suspects it will not hang around long once someone discovers a more profitable use for the property. *Author's collection.*

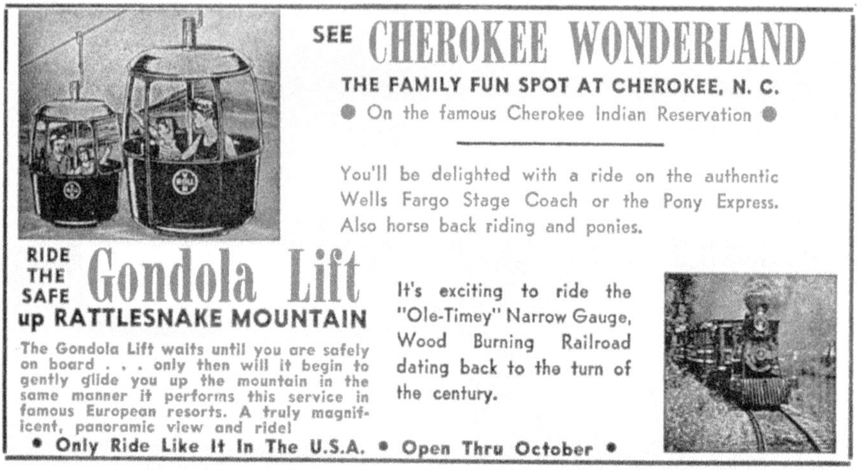

SEE CHEROKEE WONDERLAND
THE FAMILY FUN SPOT AT CHEROKEE, N. C.
● On the famous Cherokee Indian Reservation ●

You'll be delighted with a ride on the authentic Wells Fargo Stage Coach or the Pony Express. Also horse back riding and ponies.

RIDE THE SAFE Gondola Lift up RATTLESNAKE MOUNTAIN

The Gondola Lift waits until you are safely on board . . . only then will it begin to gently glide you up the mountain in the same manner it performs this service in famous European resorts. A truly magnificent, panoramic view and ride!

● Only Ride Like It In The U.S.A. ● Open Thru October ●

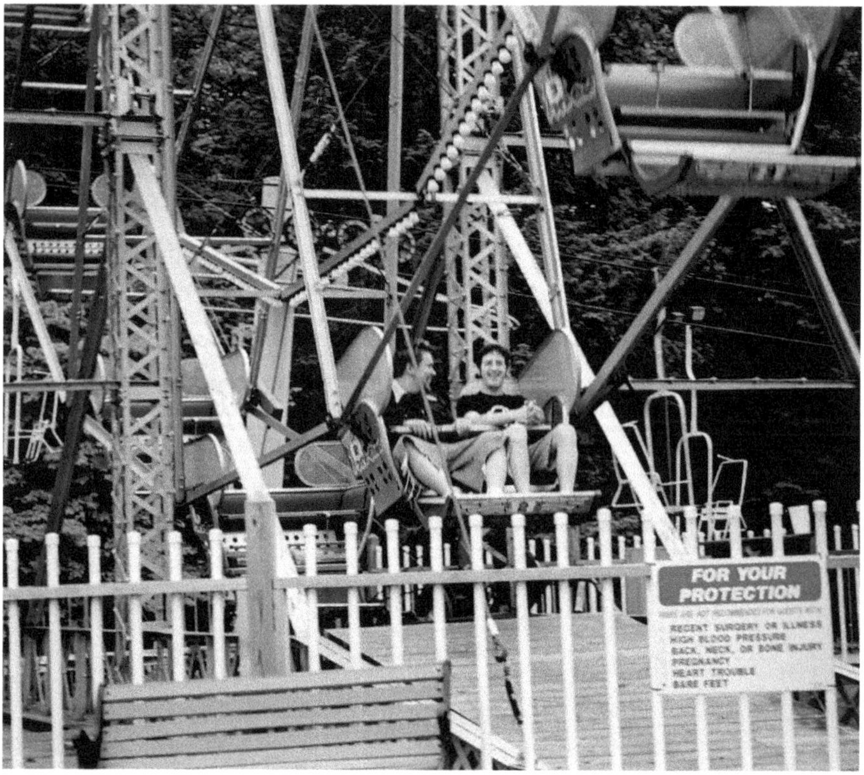

It's exciting to ride the "Ole-Timey" Narrow Gauge, Wood Burning Railroad dating back to the turn of the century.

OPPOSITE, TOP: The Cherokee Wonderland amusement park has a most obscure history, documented mainly in articles describing its closure. It seems to have been in operation from roughly 1960 to 1964, at which time the operators ceased making lease payments on the land. The final mention of Cherokee Wonderland came with the forced removal of its gondola sky lift up Rattlesnake Mountain in May 1966. *Author's collection.*

OPPOSITE, BOTTOM & ABOVE: Someone always seemed to believe that they had come up with a winning formula for a Smokies amusement park that could siphon tourists away from Dollywood, but that usually proved to be a corncob-pipe dream. Gatlinburg's Fun Mountain, dating to 1998 and with a list of activities that took up a quarter of its ad space, had an astonishingly short lifespan. Locals insist that its former site has made more as a ten-dollar public parking lot than the park ever did while in operation. *Author's collection; Brian McKnight collection.*

RIGHT: An even bigger flopparoonie was Gatlinburg Place, which sang and danced its way into town in 1981, near the former site of Homespun Valley Mountaineer Village. Two more dissimilar attractions could hardly be imagined. *Author's collection.*

OPPOSITE: It is hard to pinpoint just what Gatlinburg Place was supposed to be, and perhaps that was the whole problem. Was it an amusement park? Not exactly. Was it a theater? Only partly. Did it try to copy Disney? It had its own version of Frontierland's Country Bear Jamboree. Was it a success? Nope-a-dee-doo-dah! *Author's collection.*

THE GREATEST SHOW NEXT TO THE SMOKIES

Up, Up and Away.

The movie experience of a lifetime!
Blast off on an incredible journey into time and space with the award-winning film, "To Fly" in breathtaking IMAX on the world's largest movie screen...over seven stories tall!
Direct from the Smithsonian Institution...this exciting cinema experience will have you at the edge of your seat. It feels like you're actually there floating over thunderous Niagara Falls, racing into the darkness of space and drifting over treacherous mountains in a hang glider. Rediscover the thrill of flight in the most unique way ever...with you in the pilot's seat!

And More Thrilling Adventures
"Catch the Sun" is the second action-packed feature presentation in the spectacular IMAX Theatre. It's a thrill a minute as you feel the experience of racing boats, dipping airplanes, menacing locomotives, plunging roller coasters, speeding ice boats. Then, you'll rest your eyes on some of the most beautiful landscape ever filmed...all on a screen as big and broad as the eye can see. Come to think of it, a better name for this production would be "Catch your breath"!

ALL NEW Pop Goes America '81

The Liveliest of Live Revues!
The stage comes alive every summer evening, every weekend in the Fall, with the Gatlinburg Place Singers in a dazzling revue of song, music and dance.
This year's all-new version presents the history of America's country music in an hour-and-a-half brilliantly choreographed salute. Stunning scenery, effects and a cast of talented young performers highlight this surprise-a-minute musical spectacular that includes everything from Bluegrass to country disco. It's "stand up and cheer" quality entertainment.

It's the best evening of musical theater you'll see in Gatlinburg. Don't miss it!

First Class Shops. Browse through an impressive selection of unique gifts and mountain crafts at the Sugerlands Emporium. You'll be pleasantly surprised at the quality and value!

Eats, Treats. Tempt your tastebuds with real country eating (all summer long) at the Smokies Kitchen. For your sweet tooth...the Honey Tree offers ice cream, mountain made fudge, candy and authentic funnel cakes. Of course, you can always snack on popcorn, pizza and soft drinks at convenient food locations.

ALL NEW kid's place
Opens in June

Most energetic place in Tennessee
Only at Gatlinburg Place can your kids have such healthy fun and unique excitement.
They'll crawl, swing, jump, slide, climb their way through the happiest attraction ever staged. Let them loose to challenge the amazing Ball Crawl or Swinging Suspension Bridge to name just two of the many, many activities. There's never been anything like it in Tennessee...just for kids, just for fun!

ALL NEW
Backwoods Bear Jamboree
You'll love those crazy critters with pickin' paws.
Take your "bear's eye" seat in the wonderful Wilderness Theatre. Enjoy a knee slappin', foot stompin' musical hoe-down with the zaniest animated animals you've ever seen.
Let Zeb, Zeno, Hector and a gang of loveable bears, possums, gophers and a crow entertain you with singing and pickin' to some of the finest country music this side of the Smokies. It's an all new, all happy, greatly expanded show everybody loves.

Games. There's a challenging arcade loaded with big plushy prizes. There's remote-action boats everyone loves to steer. And, on the Gatlinburg Place Plaza there's always something happening. Take a seat and relax to the sounds of live country and Bluegrass music, or the antics of the stars of the Backwoods Bear Jamboree. There's no rush or hurry, so plan to stop by and sit a spell!

And a Plaza Full of Music and Fun!

ABOVE: Now, what is a concrete triceratops doing sitting alone along U.S. 441 in Cherokee? Anyone who might have ever had the answer now seems to be extinct. This figure has glass eyes and is solidly built with a rebar skeleton, but the answer to what sort of attraction—if any—it was originally a part of has long since gone the way of the dinosaur. *Author's collection.*

OPPOSITE: Back in chapter one, we saw the Cherokee gift shop with a parking lot full of photo-op statues. Here is that green tyrannosaurus again, with your twelve-year-old author trying to mimic its posture in 1975. Whether this dino and the previously mentioned triceratops are related is unknown; perhaps they both escaped from some long-forgotten miniature-golf course of the Cretaceous period. *Author's collection.*

OPPOSITE, TOP: Now our journey has brought us back to Pigeon Forge, where the indoor collection known as Fairyland was one of the town's earliest attractions, going back to the early 1950s. Animated dioramas ranged from traditional fairy tales to a very strange look into the wonderful world of Disney, as seen in this classic brochure. *Brian McKnight collection.*

OPPOSITE, BOTTOM: A characteristic that ran through most of Fairyland's scenes was their mixing and matching of characters from unrelated stories and nursery rhymes. Here we see a not-so-dumb-looking Simple Simon and the Pieman (on leave from Howard Johnson's, we assume) sharing space with nightshirt-clad Wee Willie Winkie. *Author's collection.*

ABOVE: Mickey Mouse and his cohorts were not the only cartoon stars to be found at Fairyland. These figures obviously started their lives as Hanna-Barbera legends Yogi Bear, Huckleberry Hound, Snagglepuss and three sets of Mr. Jinks the cat chasing Pixie and/or Dixie. *Brian McKnight collection.*

ABOVE: Fairyland closed up its workshop in the late 1970s, and its animated figures found many new owners throughout Sevier County. The former site became a Ponderosa Steakhouse, which is now a lost attraction itself. A Krispy Kreme Doughnuts stand now occupies the former Fairyland bailiwick. *Author's collection.*

OPPOSITE: Fairy folk also hung out in Cherokee in an obscure early-1970s attraction called Land of the Little People. On the second floor of a gift shop, visitors meandered through scenes depicting the Cherokee legends about leprechauns. Today, the only visible remnant of that tour is this fragment of a mural, which has survived inside a storage closet in the current gift shop operating in that space. *Skylar Spake collection.*

OPPOSITE: Jolly old St. Nicholas opened a summer branch of his North Pole workshop in Cherokee around 1966, and while it is hardly a "lost attraction," you will no longer see these examples of its entrance signage. The billboard-sized Santa dates from a couple of years after the opening; the fluorescent red and green cottage with giant waving Kringle appeared around two decades later. *Both, author's collection.*

ABOVE: The merry old gift-giver also hung out on the roof of this Santa's Cottage shop in Gatlinburg during the 1970s. It could be considered the distant ancestor of today's mega-sized Smokies stores such as the Famous Christmas Place in Pigeon Forge. *Butch Hudson collection.*

OPPOSITE: The tourist business was well known for trying anything that might make a buck, even if that meant shooting at a buck—or a replica of one, anyway. This attraction was apparently part of a chain of such sporting spots known as Realistic Ranges, but it soon disappeared back into the brush, just like its artificial Bambi. *Author's collection.*

ABOVE: Carbo's Smoky Mountain Police Museum was a Pigeon Forge fixture for many years, primarily serving as a shrine to famed Tennessee "Walking Tall" sheriff Buford Pusser. The museum was a bit cagey about which relics were real and which were props from the movie made about Pusser's controversial career. *Author's collection.*

OPPOSITE, TOP: One did not have to be Buford Pusser to feel like they were walking tall through the landscape of Lindsey Miniature Village in Maggie Valley. The pint-sized structures were fashioned with intricate detail—appropriate, since the owners were in the business of building dollhouses. *Author's collection.*

OPPOSITE, BOTTOM: Along Gatlinburg's main highway, what could have looked more out of place than a shiny giant spaceship? Well, plenty of things (as it turned out), but in the early 1960s, the Gatlinburg Space Ship prefigured the high-tech motion simulator attractions to come. Through a projected film and some custom-built hydraulics, it gave the impression of a trip to the moon and beyond, long before Apollo 11. *Joy Stout Jucker collection.*

ABOVE: There is little use in asking for more information about these two Pigeon Forge attractions, because what you see here is all that is known about them. In the days when Pigeon Forge had a combined total of 250 motel rooms, it was not very difficult to locate anything along the tourist strip of U.S. 441. *Author's collection.*

ABOVE: See, we told you the spaceship wasn't going to be the weirdest sight in Gatlinburg for long. Xanadu, meant to represent the joys of futuristic living, had one location in Kissimmee, Florida, and another in the Smokies. Despite its lurid brochures, the house of the future was a thing of the past by the early 1980s. *Author's collection.*

OPPOSITE: The Big Boy, with his checkered overalls and hoisted hamburger, had only a brief vacation in Cherokee around 2005, but if concrete dinosaurs and Santa Claus could hang out among the bears and Native Americans, so could he. *Author's collection.*

CHAPTER THREE

Kings of the Wild Frontier

Along with all the other fish-out-of-water attractions we have just seen—some quite literally featured fish in or out of the water—there was another category of "what's that doing here?" places that is major enough to deserve a chapter of its own. That, pardners, was the craze for theme parks that tried their durndest to emulate the look and feel of the Old West.

Many of the other attractions were influenced by pop culture and mass media, but none more so than the Western theme parks. They likely would not have existed at all had motion pictures not fallen in love with Western lore from their earliest days. And there probably would not have been as many of them in the 1960s had it not been for the enduring popularity of Westerns on television. Ironically, the heyday of the TV Western was already beginning its slow ride into the sunset when the Smokies' rendition of the theme began.

You will notice that while both sides of the mountains are represented here, North Carolina seemed to overshadow Tennessee in the sheer number of its Western theme parks. Perhaps the reason for this is the obvious one: while we have all heard stories about cowboys and Indians, who ever heard of a scenario featuring cowboys and hillbillies?

ABOVE: Frontier Town was apparently a somewhat premature attempt at a Western park, with little more than some exhibits of cowboy relics and an incongruous pink-and-blue-striped canopy serving some purpose. It was located in Pigeon Forge before there was much else to see there, and the angle of this postcard view hints that its site is now occupied by a motel that, at the time of this writing, is known as the Bear Mount Inn and Suites. *Author's collection.*

OPPOSITE: While the nation was in the grips of the centennial of the Civil War, the Robbins brothers—Harry, Grover and Spencer—who had made an attraction out of the Tweetsie Railroad at Blowing Rock, North Carolina, decided to set up a Tweetsie clone in Pigeon Forge and call it the Rebel Railroad. *Author's collection.*

1500 YDS.
REBEL RAILROAD

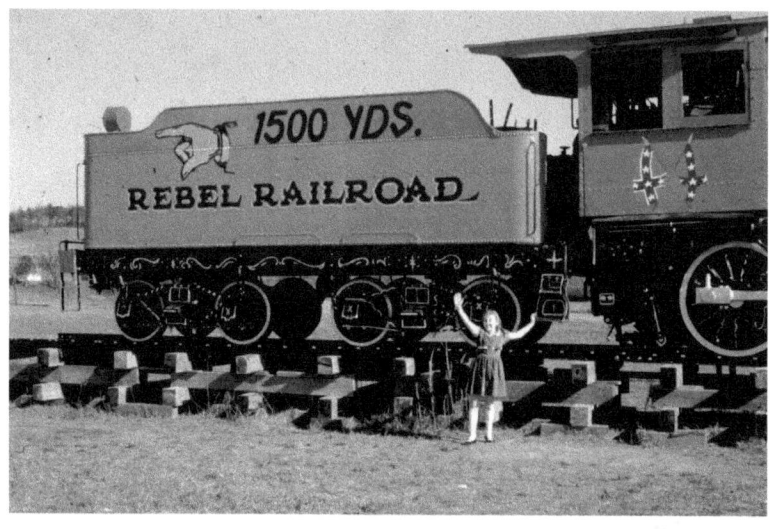

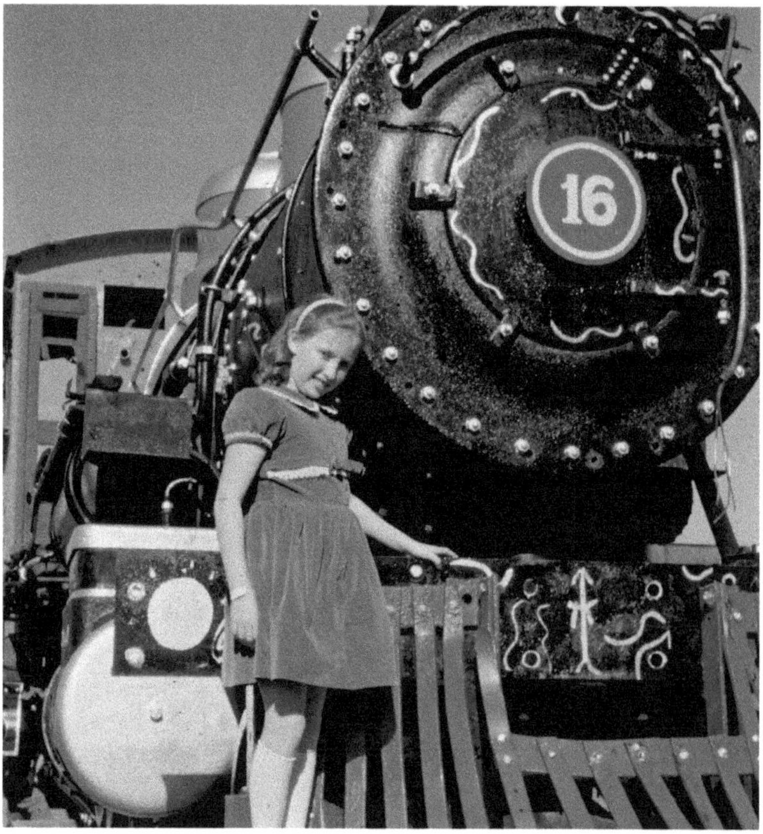
16

OPPOSITE: Young Mitzi Soward, whose family ran the Bear's Den Motel we saw earlier, preserved these beautiful color shots of the nonfunctioning locomotive at the Rebel Railroad's entrance. It is still there, even if the Rebel Railroad isn't. But we're getting ahead of our story. *Both, Mitzi Soward collection.*

ABOVE: This aerial view captures the entire Rebel Railroad park. Naturally, the main attraction was the train ride, which put a new spin on the "outlaw attacks" that were usually found in such places. Here, the Confederate train was accosted by Yankee marauders, who were quickly and comically put to rout by the Rebels. There was no question on whose side the audience's sympathies were presumed to lie. *Author's collection.*

OPPOSITE: After the Civil War centennial fever had subsided, the Rebel Railroad assumed the new identity of Goldrush Junction. This was when it truly began to shed its Confederate image for a look that matched the other Western theme parks that were bellying up to the bar in other parts of the country. *Author's collection.*

ABOVE: The Yankees having gone home—or maybe back to their baseball stadium—Goldrush Junction was able to get back to the ever-popular cowboys-versus-outlaws theme. Kids would be deputized to help march the ornery owlhoots off to jail. Reports are that, sometimes, the youngsters took their positions a little too seriously and attempted to maim their prisoners. *Author's collection.*

OPPOSITE, TOP: Goldrush Junction relied on local talent to entertain between train robberies and shootouts. Musician Osie Ownby was one of those. *Author's collection.*

OPPOSITE, BOTTOM: The general store at Goldrush Junction, like the one at Maggie Valley, looked old-fashioned but sold an assortment of souvenirs and other tourist necessities. See how many you can pick out on the shelves and in the glass cases seen here. *Author's collection.*

ABOVE: After the close of the 1964–65 New York World's Fair, Goldrush Junction snared the exposition's hit log flume ride—or at least half of it, as the remainder went to another amusement park in Florida. At the time, very few people had experienced the now-common flume ride, so it became a source of much pride for Goldrush. *Author's collection.*

ABOVE: The log flume joined the train ride and a few other park sights on this neon-colored pennant. This may well be one of the final souvenirs produced with the Goldrush Junction name, because the times were about to start a-changin' again. *Brian McKnight collection.*

OPPOSITE: During 1975–76, Goldrush Junction was purchased by Branson, Missouri tourism tycoons Jack and Pete Herschend, the brains behind that town's Silver Dollar City. For a single season, their Pigeon Forge operation labored under the somewhat awkward moniker of New Goldrush Amusement Park. *Author's collection.*

June 22 - July 28
Nightly 6-10 p.m.

We'll have different Featured Events, but one thing that's always the same is the greatest variety of country, gospel and bluegrass music and dancin' you'll find anywhere. There are multiple stage locations with performances going on simultaneously literally "filling the mountains with music!"

Special Features

June 22 - 28	Search for Talent
June 29 - July 14	National Mountain Music Festival
July 15 - 21	Clogging Cavalcade
July 22 - 28	Bluegrass Jubilee

Remember - if you enter Silver Dollar City after 3 p.m. you can return the next day FREE!

Smoky Mountain Country Getaway Guide

Located just 5 miles N. of Gatlinburg at Pigeon Forge, Tennessee

OPPOSITE: Finally, in 1977, the Herschends brought their attraction in line with home base in Branson, changing New Goldrush to Silver Dollar City. In 1986, they partnered with Sevier County's favorite daughter to transform Silver Dollar City into Dollywood. Through all its changes, the same nonfunctioning locomotive that marked the entrance to the Rebel Railroad has stood its ground by the side of U.S. 441. *Author's collection.*

ABOVE: Around the same time that the Rebel Railroad started making Yankees shake in their boots, over at Maggie Valley, former Holiday Inn franchisee R.B. Coburn opened Ghost Town in the Sky. As this early souvenir booklet shows, in the early days, it was alternatively known as Ghost Mountain Park. *Author's collection.*

OPPOSITE: When Ghost Town in the Sky opened in June 1961, its most distinctive feature was a chairlift to the Western town at the summit. Whereas most parks of its type featured a train ride, Ghost Town did not, as there was not room for it on top of the mountain. *Author's collection.*

ABOVE: Naturally, the highlight of any day at Ghost Town was when the outlaws and the marshal would have to fight it out, *Gunsmoke* style, in the street. On one such day, the photographers from the View-Master company were on hand to preserve the images in three dimensions. *Author's collection.*

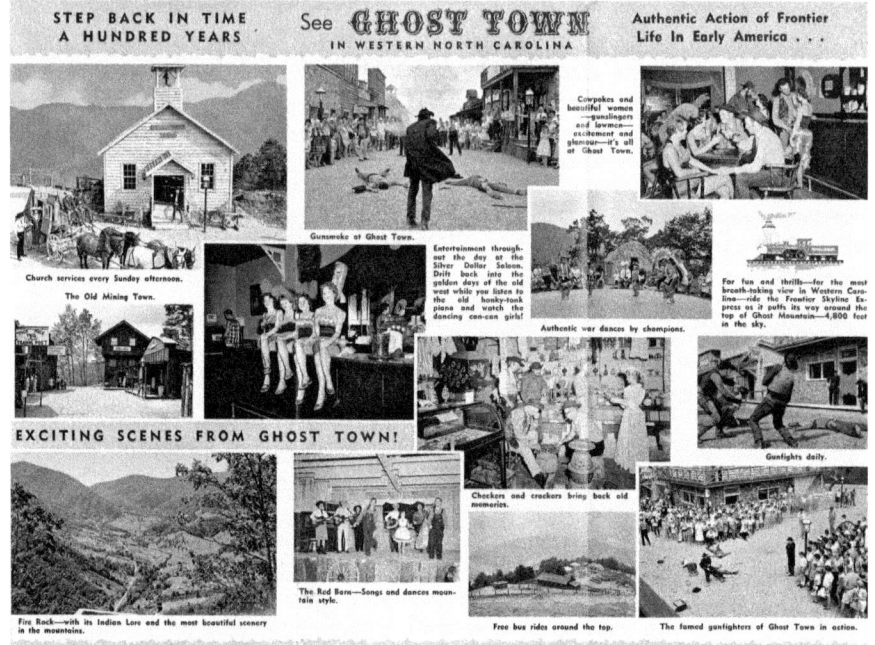

ABOVE: By the time of this remarkable spread, Ghost Town had added an incline railway to get people who were too nervous for the chairlift to the top. Also, R.B. Coburn had gone on to open an even larger Western park in Florida, the gigantic Six Gun Territory at Silver Springs. *Author's collection.*

OPPOSITE: Ghost Town in the Sky became a ghost town for real when it closed in 2002—at least for the first time. In the years since, it has reopened and shut down more than once but currently sits abandoned. This former gunslinger with his inner workings showing is on display in the antiques store adjacent to Maggie Valley Carpet Golf, patiently awaiting the ghost town's next act. *Jerry Thompson collection.*

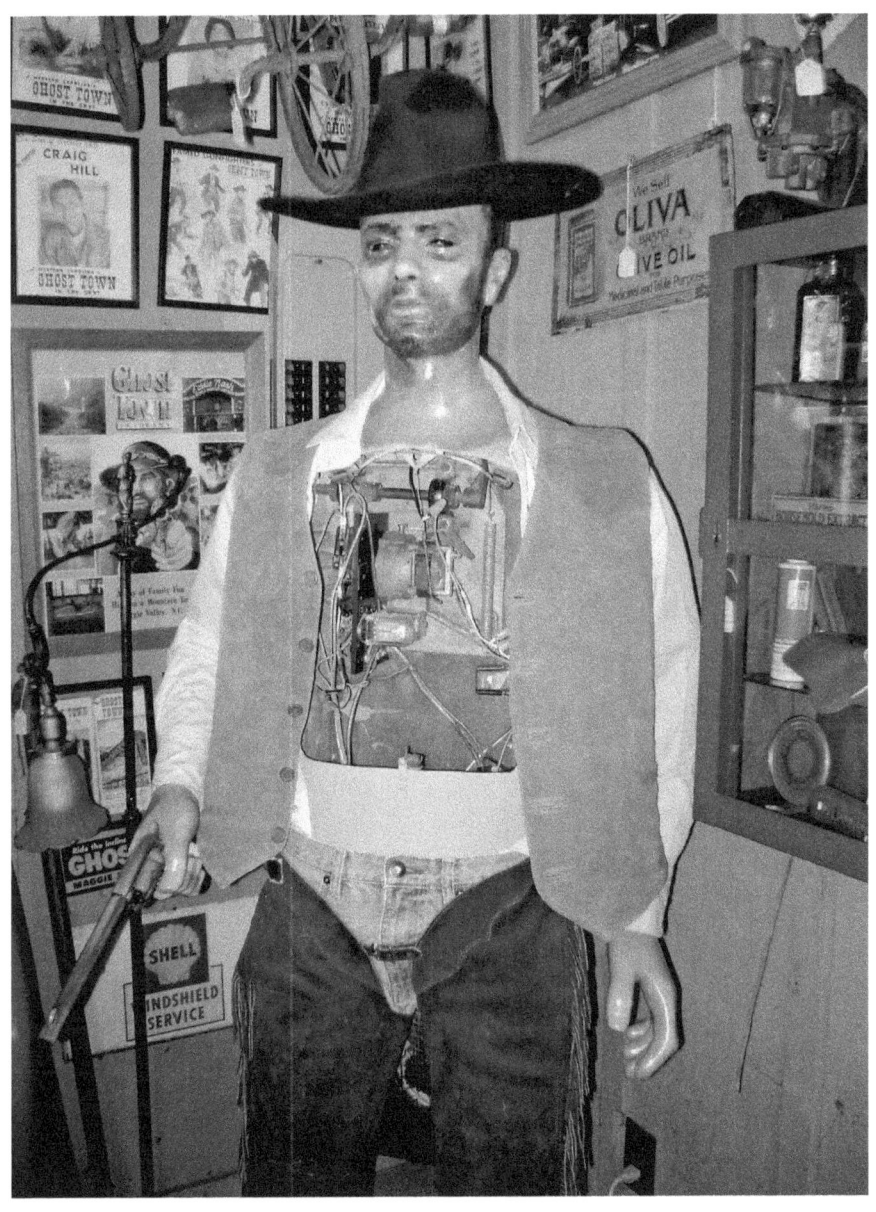

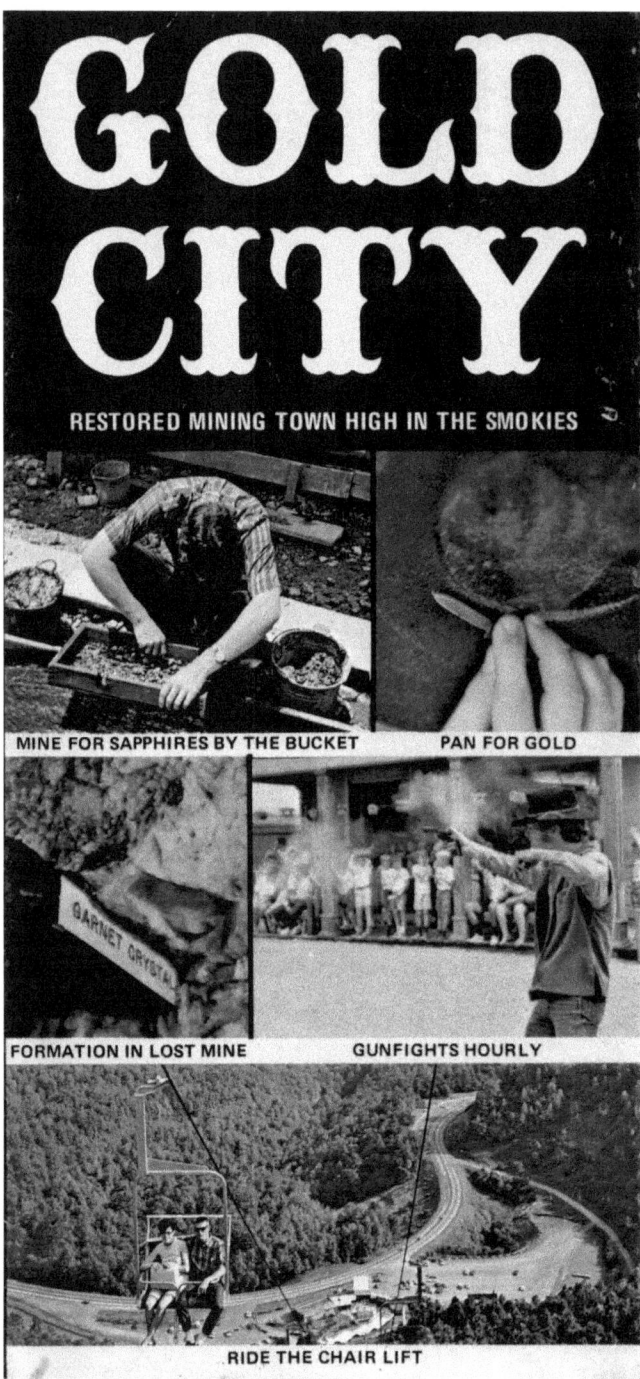

Somewhat isolated from the other mountain attractions, when Gold City at Franklin opened in 1967, it had a Spanish theme starring Hernando de Soto. Within a few years, it had said adios to the Spaniards and converted to a Western theme. Since it was on top of a mountain and accessed by chairlift, the similarity to Ghost Town in the Sky was unmistakable (and probably intentional). In recent years, Gold City has returned as a "pan for gold" roadside stop, but the Western town is long dead and buried. *Both, Jeremy Kennedy collection.*

ABOVE: The Old Smoky miniature railroad near Cherokee took what was usually the main feature of any Western park and made it the sole attraction. This postcard view captures all the fun and excitement, or perhaps the lack thereof. *Author's collection.*

OPPOSITE: After R.B. Coburn finished his Florida project at Six Gun Territory, he returned to North Carolina with another park to build. His Frontier Land in Cherokee opened in 1965, and the advertising immediately made it clear that the Plains Indians image was going to be prominent. *Author's collection.*

This amazing aerial shot documents not only the entire Frontier Land property but also many of the other attractions and businesses that surrounded it. Incredibly, the A-frame building in the lower right-hand corner survives today as the Frontier Pancake House, although it is missing its red-and-white-striped Kentucky Fried Chicken annex. It is believed that the gondola skyride that carried visitors from the parking lot to the Western town might have been the relocated one from the defunct Cherokee Wonderland. *Author's collection.*

OPPOSITE: As this early brochure indicates, Frontier Land was originally divided into three themed sections: Fort Cherokee, Pioneer Junction and Indian Territory. Later, other areas were added, including a set of amusement rides known as Frontier Funland. *Author's collection.*

ABOVE: There was one problem: With Frontier Land located on an actual reservation, how would the usual cowboys-and-Indians scenario play out, making the Native Americans the bad guys? As a response, Frontier Land made it very clear that the dastardly deeds such as this one were perpetrated by *renegade* braves, not the law-abiding members of the tribe. *Author's collection.*

ABOVE: No Western park had to make any excuses when it came time for the cancan girls in the saloon to display their undeniable charms. As with Six Gun Territory, these jobs provided gainful summer employment for high school and college students from throughout the area. *Author's collection.*

OPPOSITE, TOP: As the name would suggest, the Nashville record label known as Partheme specialized in producing vinyl LPs as souvenirs for theme parks. Besides this Frontier Land example, during its short life, Partheme also released disks commemorating Ghost Town in the Sky, Goldrush Junction, the Land of the Little People and Six Flags over Georgia, among others. *Author's collection.*

OPPOSITE, BOTTOM: By the time of this 1981 brochure, Frontier Land was nearing its journey to the happy hunting grounds. It closed in 1983, and for several years, the property was used as a water park. Today, it serves as home to Cherokee's massive Harrah's Casino, and no traces of Pioneer Junction or Frontier Funland are to be found. *Author's collection.*

CHAPTER FOUR

This Way, Please

Now we move from the ridiculous to the sublime—or at least sometimes sublime. One of the types of attractions that can be found in practically any heavily visited tourism center is the wax museum. These collections of more-or-less-lifelike effigies have been around for decades and have taken on many different forms, from the devoutly religious to its polar opposite, with many stops in between.

Actually, wax museums are not the only exhibits to pull up a rocker and make themselves at home in the hill country. Considering how many people vacation in the mountains with the intention of communing with nature, hiking and marveling at the beauty of a natural stream and the lush foliage, it is somewhat amazing how many attractions wanted to take them away from all that and coop people up in dimly-lit hallways to gaze at exhibits behind glass. But, variety provides the flavor of any tourist hot spot, and so it has been with the Smokies. Now we shall see some of the museums that we can no longer see—see?

ABOVE: Of all the wax museums, the most dignified was Christus Gardens. Founded by Ronald Ligon in August 1960, it presented major events in the life of Christ through a series of tableaux, complete with lighting and sound effects and choral music. *Author's collection.*

OPPOSITE: Outside of the wax dioramas, Christus Gardens' most famous sight was its concave marble carving of Christ's head, designed in such a way that the face seemed to turn to look at the viewer from every possible angle. *Mark Pedro collection.*

OPPOSITE, TOP: The rotunda at Christus Gardens displayed an attraction that is lost because it never existed. "Christ of the Smokies" was meant to be a one-hundred-foot-tall statue, surfaced in white enameled aluminum, to be placed atop Gatlinburg's Crockett Mountain. Had it been built, the monument would have been almost as tall as the Christ statue in Rio de Janeiro but still fifty feet shorter than the Statue of Liberty. *Mark Pedro collection.*

OPPOSITE, BOTTOM: For all its dignity, Christus Gardens was just as heavy an advertiser as any other Smokies attraction. In this shot of Bill's Rib House Restaurant, look closely under the windows and you will spy, with your little eye, two of Christus Gardens' numerous green-and-yellow wood benches. *Author's collection.*

ABOVE: At the end of 2007, Christus Gardens closed so that condominiums could be constructed on its valuable property. But the U.S. recession—or an even higher power—intervened, and the galleries reopened as Christ in the Smokies Museum in September 2009. The original 1960 figures having been sold, an all-new version of each scene was created by former caretaker Mark Pedro. Today, this Christus Gardens billboard is one of the only remnants of the original, hidden by foliage for most of the year. *Brian McKnight collection.*

RIGHT: Taking advantage of Christus Gardens' reflected glory, other religious-themed attractions came to Gatlinburg. The National Bible Museum was one of those. But as a golden rule, none of them lasted for very long. *Author's collection.*

OPPOSITE: While Christus Gardens celebrated the beauty of Jesus's life story, there was another short-lived Gatlinburg attraction that quite obviously set out to present the opposite side of the Bible, with a different star personage. The Tour through Hell might not have been the most unwanted attraction in tourism history, but it was soon sent straight to…well, you get the idea. *Author's collection.*

LEFT & OPPOSITE, TOP: Um, you thought the Tour through Hell was the ultimate in AntiChristus Gardens competition, did you? Then you have never heard of the Museum of Witchcraft and Magic. At least the Tour through Hell was intended to be a cautionary lesson. The Museum of Witchcraft not only employed all the accoutrements of the occult but also unapologetically celebrated them. *Both, Author's collection.*

OPPOSITE, BOTTOM: With Gatlinburg and the Smokies long established as a popular destination for church tours, it is difficult to imagine how those groups might have responded to this combination of devil worship and even topless women, as seen in the top row of lurid photos. The "Fun for All" claim might have been a little overdone. *Author's collection.*

OPPOSITE, TOP: Not all area museums were of the wax type. Pigeon Forge's Smoky Mountain Car Museum dated back to 1957, and instead of re-created history, it presented more than thirty actual restored antique autos. *Author's collection.*

OPPOSITE, BOTTOM: Indoors, the Smoky Mountain Car Museum contained not only the advertised vehicles but also an array of automotive-related memorabilia. This illuminated row of classic gas-pump glass globes was a real eye-pleaser; underneath the right-hand end, note one of those ubiquitous fluorescent-colored felt pennants. *Author's collection.*

ABOVE: By 2015, the Car Museum had driven away and the building sat empty, awaiting redevelopment. The leftover signage advertising Evel Knievel's motorcycle could be a clue as to how outdated its displays might have seemed to tourists of the twenty-first century. The property is now home to a much more relatable twenty-first-century sight: a Dollar General store. *Both, author's collection.*

ABOVE: In its pre-tourism days, Gatlinburg had a movie theater, just like thousands of other small towns. By the 1970s, the building had been converted into the American Historical Wax Museum, where scenes could be viewed up close rather than on a silver screen. *Author's collection.*

OPPOSITE: In a situation that would become ever more common in the tourist biz, Gatlinburg's wax museum shared ownership with other such facilities in Gettysburg and Williamsburg. Each was customized for its location, though, with notable events and personages from Tennessee depicted in the Smokies' version. *Brian McKnight collection.*

An entire section devoted to...
TENNESSEE HISTORY
HERE YOU WILL MEET FAMOUS TENNESSEANS WHO BLAZED THE WILDERNESS AND HELPED FORM OUR AMERICAN HERITAGE...

Betsy Ross and the American flag

AMERICA'S MOST REALISTIC COMPLETELY AIR CONDITIONED
WAX MUSEUM

Wax Museum Hours Open
April thru October 9 a.m. to 10 p.m.
June, July and August 8 a.m. to 11 p.m.
November thru March 9 a.m. - 5 p.m.
GROUP RATES .. Schools, Conventions, Clubs, etc.
Call 615—436-4462 or write Group Director . . .
Edna Headrick, 544 Parkway, Gatlinburg, TN 37738
Parking ½ block north, in city parking lot.

ALSO VISIT

NATIONAL CIVIL WAR WAX MUSEUM GETTYSBURG, PA.

NATIONAL WILLIAMSBURG WAX MUSEUM WILLIAMSBURG, VIRGINIA

Printed in U.S.A.

Gatlinburg's
AMERICAN HISTORICAL
WAX MUSEUM

General of the Armies, Dwight D. Eisenhower

On The Parkway
Gatlinburg, Tennessee
OPEN DAILY - ALL YEAR - Including Sunday

ABOVE: The American Historical Wax Museum advertised its range as "From Columbus to the Astronauts," and that covered a lot of ground—as well as outer space. Most of the usual historical events could be found among its dioramas, but also some odd concepts. Among the vignettes seen here is Huckleberry Finn meeting his curmudgeonly creator, Mark Twain. *Author's collection.*

OPPOSITE, TOP: Stars over Gatlinburg was somewhat of a "sequel" to the American Historical Wax Museum in that it highlighted the celebrities whose careers had not played such an important part in the history of the country but whose roles in popular culture were undeniable. The results, as illustrated here, were uneven (to put it kindly). *Author's collection.*

OPPOSITE, BOTTOM: The fact that so many of the Stars over Gatlinburg figures bore little or no resemblance to the celebrities they were supposed to depict had its advantages. Years after the museum's closure, some of these same figures have returned to Gatlinburg, particularly at the Christ in the Smokies Museum, where they take on new roles as disciples or Roman soldiers or other biblical characters. *Author's collection.*

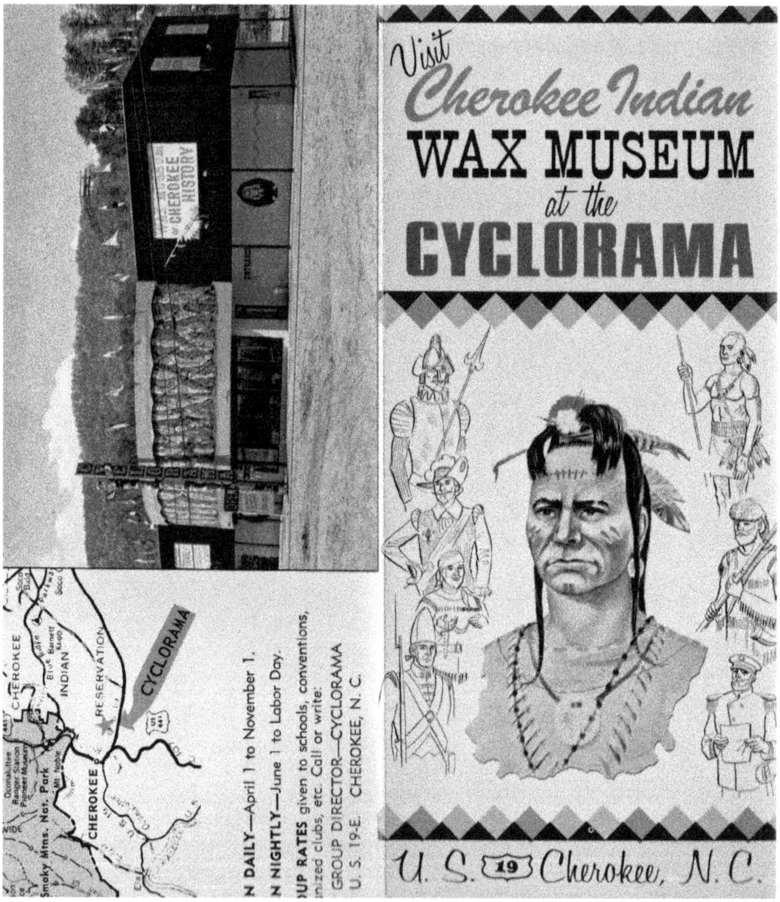
Visit
Cherokee Indian
WAX MUSEUM
at the
CYCLORAMA
U. S. 19 Cherokee, N. C.
CYCLORAMA
CHEROKEE
INDIAN
RESERVATION
N DAILY—April 1 to November 1.
N NIGHTLY—June 1 to Labor Day.
UP RATES given to schools, conventions,
nized clubs, etc. Call or write:
GROUP DIRECTOR—CYCLORAMA
U. S. 19-E CHEROKEE, N. C.
CHEROKEE HISTORY

Ripley's
Believe It or Not!
MUSEUM

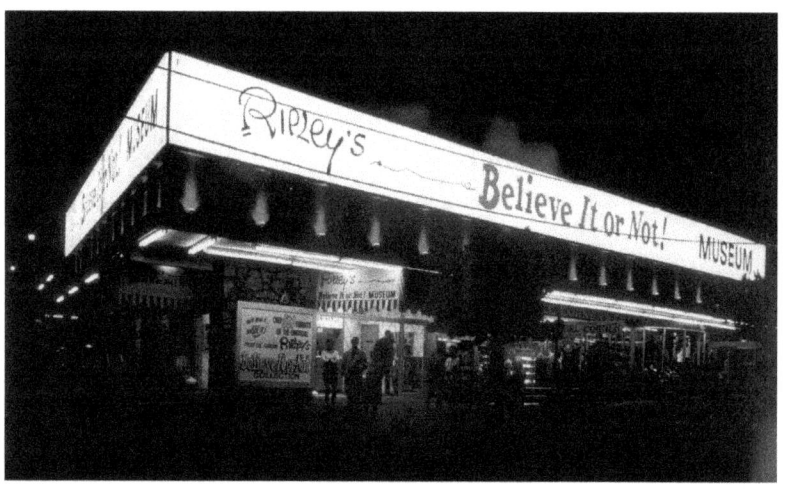

HISTORY RECREATED IN CANDY
Only at Ripley's Believe It Or Not! Museum could you ever hope to see a scale model as spectacular as the CIRCUS MAXIMUS, the great Roman amphitheatre where thousands of Christians met their death in the days of Emperor Nero. The replica was created with unbelievable artistry by Laszlo Dorogi, famed Las Vegas Pastry Chef — out of 100 lbs. of Icing Sugar!

LINCOLN'S LOG CABIN
This unusual replica of our great President's humble birthplace was awarded a special citation for the most outstanding exhibit at the American Numismatic Convention of 1961. In total it weighs over 175 lbs. and in case you're in no mood for counting, we can tell you . . . it contains 9,500 uncirculated Lincoln pennies.

WALK THRU THE WORLD'S STRANGEST GRAVEYARD
Robert Ripley was the first Journalist of importance to catalog and publish the curious epitaphs that some people have mounted over the graves of their "Dearly Departed". At the Ripley Museum you can read for yourself the best of these fascinating and humorous epitaphs found in sobriety of graveyards throughout the world.

THERE REALLY WAS A MOTHER GOOSE
Children have always known it . . . now here is proof for adults too. Her maiden name was Elizabeth Foster and she married Isaac Goose in 1692. When you learn how many children she had you'll know why she wrote nursery rhymes.

CANNIBAL CURIO
There are only three examples of this rare oddity in America, and Ripley's have two of them. If you are one of those people who believe only what they can see, take the opportunity to visit Gatlinburg's Believe It Or Not! Museum and see this Human Ceremonial Skull from Dutch New Guinea.

SHIP OF BONES
What most people discard, Chef Johann Zellweger transforms into ships like the Santa Maria, pictured here. Osseous (Bony) Sculpture would be an accurate description of such artworks, since they are made up entirely of chicken and turkey bones!

THE TWO-HEADED CALF
Malformed in whole or part, such unfortunate creatures were once regarded as something of supernatural origin and were referred to as "Monsters". No less an authority than Dr. C. H. Forthman, of Oklahoma, witnessed the birth of this exhibit.

THE WORLD'S SMALLEST VIOLIN
Beautifully toned, only 5½" long. Though size limits volume, this hand crafted replica was actually played by its maker on Ripley's radio show.

THE MAN OF CHAINS
This curious fellow also known as the "Jingling Fakir" is just one of many characters reproduced life-size from Ripley's world famous pocket books. He is shown complete with his groaning load of 670 lbs. which he dragged through the streets of Lahore, India.

OPPOSITE, TOP: The term "cyclorama" usually refers to a circular painting, such as the famous one in Atlanta. Cherokee's Cyclorama Wax Museum used the name indiscriminately, applying it to a normal succession of scenes depicting the history of the Cherokee tribe, both in and out of North Carolina. *Mark Pedro collection.*

OPPOSITE, BOTTOM: Today, the Ripley organization operates numerous Sevier County attractions, ranging from museums to theaters to miniature-golf courses. But it all started when the Ripley's Believe It or Not! Museum opened in Gatlinburg in 1969. This was the original building, which is now long gone; on the right-hand side, note how the museum overlapped with the Rebel Corner gift shop. This would later prove to be significant to its story. *Author's collection.*

ABOVE: In 1992, a fire that began in the Rebel Corner completely destroyed the original Ripley's museum. These were some of the better-known displays that were lost to the fire, although some were capable of being re-created later. The museum has gone through several different structures of varying designs since then and continues to suspend visitors' disbelief today. *Author's collection.*

With all of those other wild, wacky and wonderful attractions to be sampled, how many families could have been expected to give up valuable vacation time to visit Sciential, the World of Science? Apparently not many, as even longtime tourism folks in the area have no memory of it. *Author's collection.*

CHAPTER FIVE
Putt It There, Pal

As with museums, wax and otherwise, most tourist centers sought to entertain visitors of all ages with increasingly elaborate miniature-golf courses. Some of the Smokies' vintage examples, including Hillbilly Golf in Gatlinburg and Maggie Valley Carpet Golf just down the street from the ghost town that was once Ghost Town, have survived into the present day and have become landmarks. The ones we are about to visit in this chapter were not among the fortunate few.

There is no need to deny the fact that when the hill country got its first taste of the late-1950s/early-1960s style of "concrete dinosaur" course, the inspiration was Florida's beaches of the Panhandle, known popularly as the Miracle Strip. Careful observation of the approach alongside those white sands produced Gatlinburg's Jolly Golf in 1961, and it in turn begat an entire prehistoric industry for its founders.

Dinosaurs were not the only creatures roaming the Smokies' mini-golfs. Our aforementioned old traveling companions—bears, hillbillies and Indians—could also be found puttering around, as well as some other characters who were more recent arrivals. Considering the name, it is ironic that today miniature golf is bigger than ever, with courses in the Smokies that approach theme-park appearances in their landscaping and decoration. There was, however, a simpler time—just turn the page and see.

ABOVE: Two businessmen from Murfreesboro, Richard Craddock and Jim Sidwell, opened Jolly Golf at the extreme northern end of Gatlinburg in 1961. They had done their research during a trip to Florida's Miracle Strip the previous year and brought that style of miniature golf to the Smokies for the first time. *Becky Craddock collection.*

OPPOSITE: Although he ran a furniture store as a vocation, Jim Sidwell discovered that he had an uncanny knack for sculpting dinosaurs. Here he is prior to the opening of Jolly Golf, putting the finishing touches on the course's original tyrannosaurus. (There would be at least two replacements over the next forty years.) *Becky Craddock collection.*

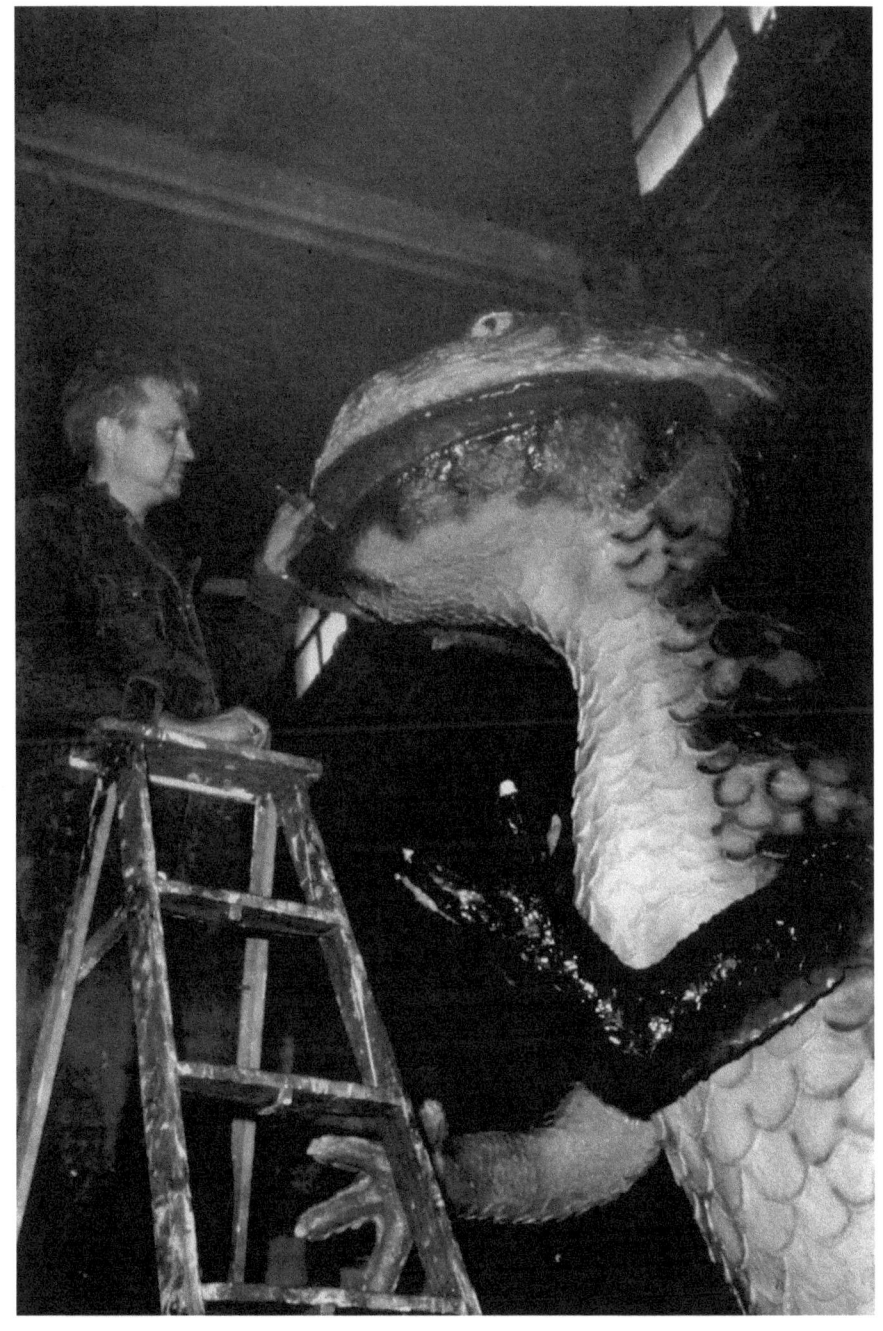

LOST ATTRACTIONS OF THE SMOKY MOUNTAINS

OPPOSITE, TOP: Sidwell's furniture warehouse became the "studio" for building the Jolly Golf figures. Here we see Shirley Craddock posing with a newly birthed dimetrodon, but immediately behind her head, note that classic Motorola television sign taking a break from the furniture store. *Becky Craddock collection.*

OPPOSITE, BOTTOM: Here is the dimetrodon after installation at Jolly Golf, with at least two other lost attractions captured by the photographer: the arrow pointing the way to Mystery Hill, and the red-and-white telephone booth that is now as extinct as the dimetrodon. *Becky Craddock collection.*

ABOVE: Although Jolly Golf started out as a single eighteen-hole course, after Richard Craddock moved on to other business ventures, Sidwell continued to expand. He also kept creating new figures, including this hairy ape. And be sure to note the plaid logo of the Econo Lodge across the street, with its thrifty Scotsman logo. *John Margolies collection.*

Jolly Golf originally had a giant Smokey Bear as one of its obstacles, with a right hand that waved. Later, the U.S. Forest Service raised objections over an unlicensed use of its trademark, and Smokey was rehabbed into "Old Pokey Bear," with a hillbilly hat and black fur. By this time, Jolly Golf had grown to two eighteen-hole courses, and the statuary continued to multiply. *Becky Craddock collection; author's collection.*

ABOVE: By the time of this November 2000 photo, Jolly Golf had been changed to Dinosaur Golf, and any nonprehistoric figures (including Smokey/Pokey) were removed. Within five years, the entire property would be razed for today's spiffy Davy Crockett Mini-Golf, a project of the Ripley organization. *Author's collection.*

OPPOSITE, TOP: In 1971, Jim Sidwell began expanding his dinosaur universe beyond the mini-golf realm. The fence from the former Fort Weare Game Park was still standing in Pigeon Forge when Sidwell began constructing a giant concrete volcano over and around it—the first phase of his Magic World theme park. *Katie Sidwell collection.*

OPPOSITE, BOTTOM: When completed, Magic World certainly did not look like anything else in Pigeon Forge. It did, however, bear a not-too-subtle resemblance to another Miracle Strip attraction, Panama City Beach's Jungle Land, which was also housed in a volcano. *Author's collection.*

LOST ATTRACTIONS OF THE SMOKY MOUNTAINS

UNBELIEVABLE
the Magnificent Journey thru
Magic World

- CAVEMAN CITY
- GHOST GROTTO
- DRAGON TRAIN RIDE
- DINOSAUR CANYON
- INVISIBLE PEOPLE
- UNDERWATER WORLD AQUARIUM
- ABOMINABLE SNOWMAN

OPPOSITE: Naturally, one of Sidwell's now-famous miniature-golf courses was a feature of Magic World. Strangely, photos of it are as scarce as living dinosaurs today; this brochure gives us our only real peek at this "add-on" attraction. *Author's collection.*

ABOVE: Like any theme park worth its theming, Magic World came with its own costumed mascot. Dizzy Dinosaur hung out around the entrance, the very sight of him being enough to make kids' heads swim. The true scale of Sidwell's latest creations can be gauged by the humongous fluorescent brontosaurus looming behind Dizzy and his young fans. *Author's collection.*

OPPOSITE, TOP: Magic World contained a garden that could also have been viewed as the showroom for Jim Sidwell's mini-golf statuary. The Dragon Train took riders on a peril-filled journey through the fiberglass monsters, complete with recorded narration and sound effects. *Author's collection.*

OPPOSITE, BOTTOM: As the years progressed, Magic World expanded beyond its prehistoric theme and encompassed many other types of entertainment. Magic shows by Merlin Rainbow were surefire crowd-pleasers—especially the stunt shown here—but the park packed much more live entertainment and rides than one would expect into its rather limited space. *Author's collection.*

ABOVE: In 1977, Magic World introduced its animatronic bear, General Cornelius Bearpatch, a creation of artist Billy Bob Irving. Irving would later win immortality for his work on the robotic entertainment for the Showbiz Pizza Place restaurant chain. *Katie Sidwell collection.*

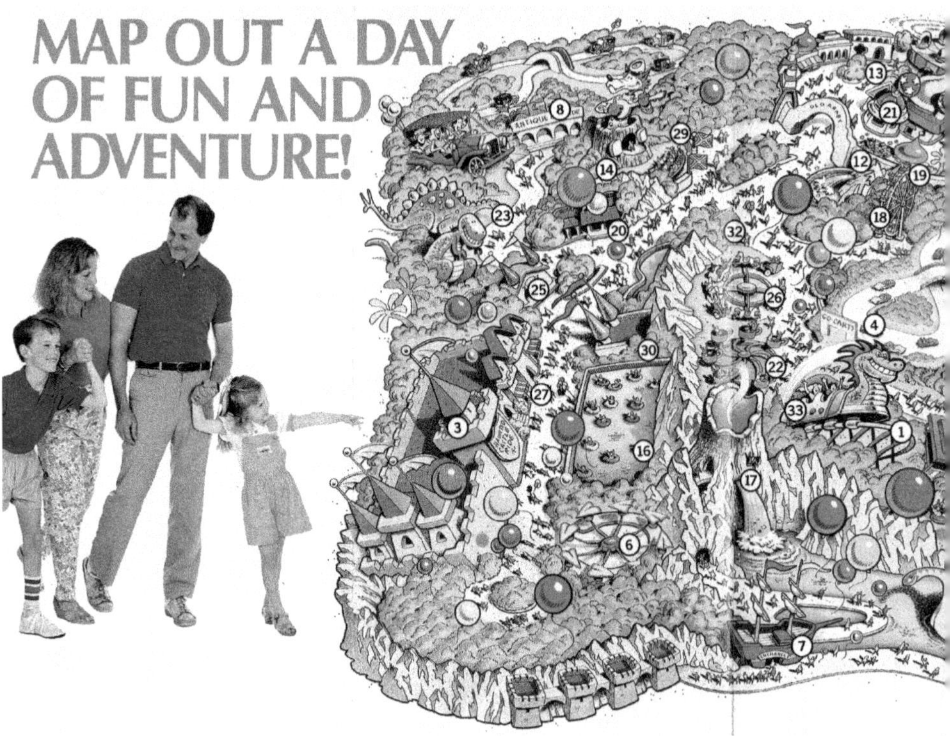

MAP OUT A DAY OF FUN AND ADVENTURE!

ATTRACTIONS

1. Dragon Coaster Ride
2. Crawling Maze
3. Haunted Castle Ride
4. New Family Go-Carts
5. Magic Carpet Ride
6. Red Baron Ride
7. Pirate Ship
8. Antique Car Ride
9. Net Climb
10. Air Bounce
11. Super Slides
12. Ball Swim
13. Crawl-a-pillar
14. Confederate Critter Show
15. Tilt-a-Whirl Ride
16. Bumper Boats
17. Volcano Walk
18. Ferris Wheel Ride
19. Restrooms
20. Snack Bar
21. Ice Cream Shop
22. Teacup Ride
23. Dinosaur Museum
24. Punching Bags
25. Live Fish Pond
26. Pony Cart Ride
27. Castle Gift Shop
28. Clyde the Camel Show
29. Family Picnic Area
30. Photo Shop
31. Giant Spider Ride
32. Information Booth
33. Mr. Frog

The panoramic overview shows Magic World as it appeared in 1985, the centerpiece volcano overshadowed by amusements of every other type. The map dates from 1992, by which time there seemed to be nowhere else to place anything new. It would not last: Magic World took a bow and disappeared at the end of its 1995 operating season. *Both, author's collection.*

ABOVE: The Sidwell family continues to operate Professor Hacker's Lost Treasure Mini-Golf on about two-thirds of the former Magic World property. In a far back corner of the lot, this former track for the antique auto ride is one of the last visible remnants of the theme park; in the center of the pavement, note the scars that once held the ride's metal guide bar. *Author's collection.*

OPPOSITE: Adventure Golf was another chain operated by the Sidwells, with locations in several states. The one in Pigeon Forge was directly across the street from Magic World and outlasted its theme-park cousin by twenty years, being razed in late 2015. *Both, author's collection.*

OPPOSITE, TOP: Contrary to what one might have been led to believe up to this point, not all miniature-golf courses in the Smokies were Sidwell family projects. Smoky Bear Golf, just a few steps away from Adventure Golf, presented a decidedly lower-tech approach. *John Margolies collection.*

OPPOSITE, BOTTOM: This melancholy-looking frog at Smoky Bear Golf seems to be Kermit's homely brother Egbert, who remained behind in obscurity while his handsomer sibling rose to the fame and stardom he still enjoys today. *John Margolies collection.*

ABOVE: Among the latter-day miniature-golf courses that have come and gone was Pigeon Forge's Firehouse Golf, where the grounds were enlivened by *Song of the South*–type bears and other wildlife carrying out their first-responder duties. The location is now home to the Lumberjack Feud show. *Author's collection.*

OPPOSITE: The national chain of Putt-Putt Golf courses set up locations in Gatlinburg, Maggie Valley and Cherokee, the one seen here from above. A Holiday Inn currently occupies the spot. The building at the top of the photo is the aforementioned Cyclorama of the Cherokee Indian wax museum; that spot is now part of parking for Harrah's Casino. *Author's collection.*

ABOVE: One of those stranger-than-fiction tales involves Pigeon Forge's Bunnyland Mini-Golf, where players putted among cages of live rabbits. The bunnies met an unfortunate and hare-raising end when they were all found slaughtered one morning. The exact circumstances are still a matter of debate among locals. *Author's collection.*

Bunnyland had been gone from the Bunny Trail for more than a dozen years when this photo was taken in 2010. The giant rabbit head used to promote the course (seen atop a van in the previous photo) sat in an overgrown lot behind the property, being slowly reclaimed by foliage. *Author's collection.*

CHAPTER SIX
A Dramatic Conclusion

In our final chapter, we take a look at a couple of themes that once had seemingly bright futures but for the most part burned out like an overworked bulb on Broadway. Both involved live performances but took completely different approaches.

Like dinosaur-themed miniature-golf courses, the outdoor drama was a product of the 1950s and 1960s. Perhaps because of the more consistent weather and longer tourism seasons in the South, outdoor dramas particularly thrived there. Some are still being performed today, but audiences have generally evinced a preference for air-conditioning as opposed to sitting in an amphitheater on a sticky summer night.

For a brief time in the 1990s and early 2000s, it appeared that the strip of U.S. 441 that ran through Sevierville and Pigeon Forge was poised to become the next Branson, Missouri, that well-known bastion of celebrity theaters. An amazing number of stars from all branches of showbiz set up their acts in the Smokies, only to find that, unlike Branson, where the shows were the main draw, there was too much competition from other types of attractions to lure tourists. One by one, the stars returned to whatever firmament had brought them, and live shows settled into their present-day form of fitting in with their neighbors rather than trying to outdo them with glitz and glamour.

OPPOSITE: Despite all attempts to learn more about it, the outdoor drama *The Great Smokies*, its Gatlinburg venue known as the Smokyland Theatre and its author Delmar Baxter have all managed to remain mysteries. It is not even certain what years marked the beginning and end of its performances. *Author's collection.*

ABOVE: Virtually everything you will ever learn about *The Great Smokies* is in this brochure. Apparently, it was cast with local talent, some of whom are still legends (such as Wiley Oakley). The whole thing really resembles Homespun Valley Mountaineer Village turned into a stage show. *Author's collection.*

OPPOSITE: The most famous of the Smokies' outdoor dramas, *Unto These Hills*, premiered in Cherokee in July 1950. Author Kermit Hunter wove together scenes from several centuries of Cherokee history, from the arrival of white explorers—causing the justifiably tense expressions seen here—to the infamous Trail of Tears, all interspersed with tribal dances and other music. *Author's collection.*

ABOVE: In this *Unto These Hills* scene, Chief Junaluska saves the life of General Andrew Jackson. Once Jackson became president of the United States, he repaid Junaluska by ordering all Cherokees removed from their ancestral lands. While a pageant titled *Unto These Hills* is still being performed, the Kermit Hunter script was nixed in 2006 in favor of a more enlightened celebration of Cherokee culture. *Author's collection.*

ABOVE & OPPOSITE, TOP: Playwright Kermit Hunter tried his pen at history on the Tennessee side of the hills with his 1957 drama *Chucky Jack*. As this colorful comic book–style handout indicates, the play was a biography of John Sevier, the first governor of Tennessee. Artist Bill Dyer was a longtime cartoonist for the *Knoxville News-Sentinel* and worked on the nationally syndicated comic strips *Oaky Doaks* and *The Adventures of Patsy*. Both, Mark Pedro collection.

OPPOSITE, BOTTOM: *Chucky Jack* had a unique way of getting paying customers to its outdoor amphitheater. A miniature train tootled around the Gatlinburg streets, picking up audience members and depositing them at the gate. While it's picking up more tourists, enjoy this view of a Kodak store and those vintage Phillips 66 gas pumps. *Loren "Yogi" Jones collection.*

Smoky Mountain Passion Play

Outdoor Drama of Jesus at Townsend, Tenn. June 11 - August 28, 1982, Monday - Saturday.
"Intense and powerful . . . unsurpassed . . . heartstopping . . ." - Knoxville News-Sentinel

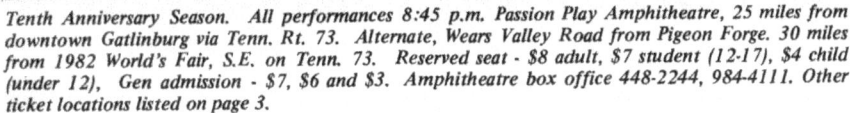

Tenth Anniversary Season. All performances 8:45 p.m. Passion Play Amphitheatre, 25 miles from downtown Gatlinburg via Tenn. Rt. 73. Alternate, Wears Valley Road from Pigeon Forge. 30 miles from 1982 World's Fair, S.E. on Tenn. 73. Reserved seat - $8 adult, $7 student (12-17), $4 child (under 12), Gen admission - $7, $6 and $3. Amphitheatre box office 448-2244, 984-4111. Other ticket locations listed on page 3.

The community of Townsend began the tradition of a Passion play in 1972, and the original run lasted until 1992. It was then revived for various periods until 2009, when the property containing its outdoor venue was sold. It would certainly not be the last time the life of Christ would be presented with living actors rather than the wax dioramas of Christus Gardens. *Mark Pedro collection; author's collection.*

ABOVE: From many pages ago, remember the artificial lake that was the locale for Tommy Bartlett's Water Circus? Well, after that enterprise was finished, the lake was filled in and turned into a model of Jerusalem the length of three football fields. Here, Mark Pedro stands in front of the construction, which was to be home to yet another Passion play. *Mark Pedro collection.*

OPPOSITE: Sevier County's newest Passion play was to be just one feature in an ambitious complex known as Kingdom Resort. Most of what was to comprise the resort never made it off the drawing board, other than a motel and the Passion play atop the former Bartlett water-ski lake. *Mark Pedro collection.*

ABOVE: With a nightly cast of some 250 actors, the Passion play at Kingdom Resort seemed too big to fail. But that is just what it did, running only from May to August 1988. In this impressive view, note the darkened horizontal window at far right; it was where the Last Supper scene would be staged in a close approximation of the famous painting. *Mark Pedro collection.*

OPPOSITE: The production housed in Pigeon Forge's Miracle Theater somewhat resembled a Passion play reimagined as a Broadway spectacle. This brochure shows some of the participants who were not all drawn accurately from biblical sources. With crowds of angels, villains and animals—among others—it was something of a miracle that it lasted from 2006 to 2010. *Author's collection.*

ABOVE: One of the earliest venues for live music along the Pigeon Forge strip was the Music Barn, home to Bill Owens. His reputation as an entertainer was soon overshadowed by that of his niece Dolly Parton, but he could hardly be faulted for that. Heavily remodeled, the building now serves as a gift shop. *Author's collection.*

OPPOSITE: No doubt the most visible celebrity in Sevier County in the 1970s and early 1980s was *Grand Ole Opry* and *Hee Haw* comedian Archie Campbell. Beginning in a conference room at Gatlinburg's Ramada Inn, Campbell and his cast would migrate from one facility to the next, growing larger each time. *Jeremy Kennedy collection.*

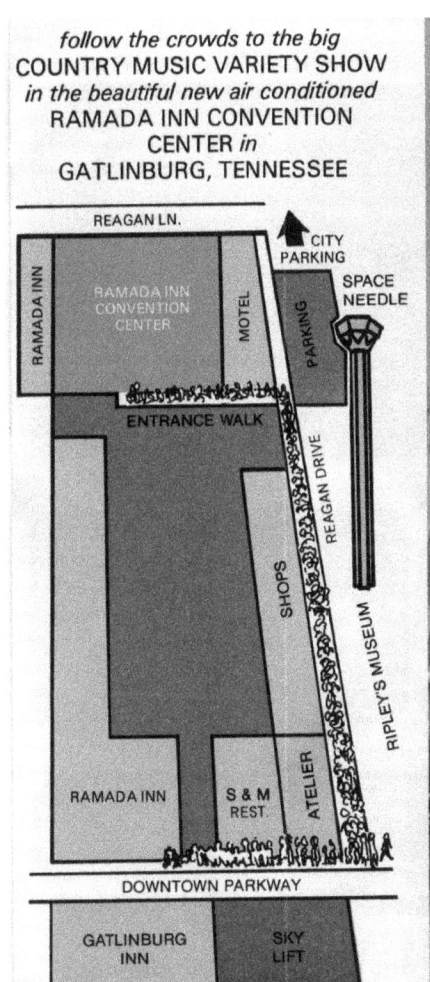

ABOVE & OPPOSITE, TOP: In 1981, Archie Campbell's wandering stopped when he opened Hee Haw Village, a small theme park along the Pigeon Forge strip. Comical cartoon buildings duplicated the sets of the syndicated Hee Haw TV show, and visitors were greeted by a statue of Campbell driving a wagon pulled by the program's trademark donkey. *Both, author's collection.*

OPPOSITE, BOTTOM: Archie Campbell and his fellow comics, stooges and musicians performed in a barn-shaped theater at the back of the property. After Campbell's death in 1987, his son Phil kept the show going for a few more years, but in 1996, the property became the site of today's Comedy Barn, a true landmark of the Pigeon Forge strip. *Author's collection.*

BONNIE LOU & BUSTER
"Jim Walter Homes" Television Show

Direct from the stage of the Grand Ole Opry — Mr. "Talk Back Trembling Lips" Ernie Ashworth

Enjoy Country Music at its Best! Recording & Television Personalities along with GRAND OLE OPRY STARS!
8:30 Nightly
Air Conditioned • Free Parking

COLISEUM
PIGEON FORGE, TENNESSEE

Genuine Mountain, Bluegrass, and Gospel Music — Comedy
Phone (615) 453-9590

Bonnie Lou and Buster might not have enjoyed the lasting national fame of Archie Campbell, but their Smoky Mountain Hayride was a fixture of local TV in eastern Tennessee for decades, sponsored by Jim Walter Homes. Beginning in 1972, their Pigeon Forge stage show entertained for more than fifteen years. *Both, author's collection.*

OPPOSITE: The Music Mansion lived up to its name as one of the first huge, ornate theaters on the Pigeon Forge strip when it opened in 1994. Even though it was a project of the Herschend family, of Silver Dollar City and Dollywood renown, somehow it just did not catch on. After closing in 1998, the building was briefly home to controversial entertainer Anita Bryant before being converted into today's Wonderworks attraction, with its upside-down façade. *Author's collection.*

ABOVE: Lee Greenwood was proud to be an American but probably not so proud of the short run of his namesake theater. Part of the problem was that it sat too far north of then-current development when it opened in 1996, closer to I-40 than the U.S. 441 strip. It closed in 2001 and was converted into a church in 2007. *Author's collection.*

ABOVE, LEFT: With the long-established popularity of the Smokies' native bears, it is somewhat surprising that it took until 2003 for anything resembling the Black Bear Jamboree to make its appearance. Even with the help of animatronic bruins, the show lasted only until 2010. Appropriately, the bear motif was replaced with a hillbilly theme, as the building now houses the noisy Hatfield-McCoy Dinner Feud ruckus. *Author's collection.*

ABOVE, RIGHT: Louise Mandrell's theater was actually more successful than most, and reports are that Mandrell's warmth and conviviality made her very popular among the locals. Her run lasted from 1997 to 2005, and even then it did not end because of lack of business. Her husband's poor health necessitated a move back to Nashville, and this brochure announced the final curtain. *Author's collection.*

OPPOSITE: Finally, we come to Elwood Smooch's Old Smoky Hoedown, starring former Ringling Bros. circus clown and comedian of many faces Billy Baker. The goofy, rubber-faced Smooch was only one of Baker's many characterizations, and combining the proven formula of country comedy, music and a bit of gospel, it kept audiences stompin' for more from 1999 until 2006. *Author's collection.*

One thing is for sure: whether you return to the Smokies every year or it's a decade between visits, on each trip, you can count on old attractions having disappeared and new ones having taken their place. There is no end to the story, only a continuation. Y'all come back now—an' don't fergit ta bring yore wallet! *Jeremy Kennedy collection.*

Bibliography

Bennett, Rod. "Stranger Than You Think: Ripley's Believe It or Not!" *Wonder Magazine* (Summer 1996).

Cotham, Steve. *Great Smoky Mountains National Park*. Charleston, SC: Arcadia Publishing, 2006.

Edge, Lynn. "Classy Mandrell to End Her Run." *Birmingham News*, July 3, 2005.

Harkins, Anthony. *Hillbilly: A Cultural History of an American Icon*. New York: Oxford University Press, 2004.

Hollis, Tim. *Dixie before Disney: 100 Years of Roadside Fun*. Jackson: University Press of Mississippi, 1999.

———. *The Land of the Smokies: Great Mountain Memories*. Jackson: University Press of Mississippi, 2007.

Hollis, Tim, and Mitzi Soward. *Lost Attractions of Sevier County*. Charleston, SC: Arcadia Publishing, 2011.

King, Veta Wilson. *Pigeon Forge*. Charleston, SC: Arcadia Publishing, 2010.

Leiper, Bart. *The Story of Gatlinburg's Christus Gardens*. Gatlinburg, TN: Christus Biblical Gardens, 1967.

Long, Travis. "Chiefly for the Tourists." *Charlotte [NC] News-Observer*, September 4, 2005.

Mountain Visitor. "James Sidwell, Dinosaur Man." June 15, 1981.

———. "New Addition in Golf Available in Pigeon Forge." June 15, 1981.

———. "New 1981 Tommy Bartlett's Water Circus." June 15, 1981.

———. "What's New at Magic World?" July 17, 1978.

Southern Living. "Outdoor Dramas Re-Create History." July 1966.

Starnes, Richard D. *Creating the Land of the Sky: Tourism and Society in Western North Carolina*. Tuscaloosa: University of Alabama Press, 2005.

Trout, Ed. *Gatlinburg: Cinderella City*. Pigeon Forge, TN: Griffin Graphics, 1984.

Zimmerman, Elena Irish. *Sevierville, Gatlinburg and Maryville*. Charleston, SC: Arcadia Publishing, 1996.

About the Author

Tim Hollis has written thirty-three books on pop culture history, a number of them concerning southeastern tourism. He also operates his own museum of vintage toys, souvenirs and other pop-culture artifacts near Birmingham, Alabama.

Visit us at
www.historypress.com

www.ingramcontent.com/pod-product-compliance
Lightning Source LLC
Chambersburg PA
CBHW040251170426
43191CB00018B/2371